MISHAL HUSAIN is one of the presenters of BBC Radio 4's
ntial *Today* programme and the news on BBC One.
years as a journalist she has worked on interna-
well as British stories and made critically
d documentaries. Her work has taken her from
Rohingya refugee camps and from interviewing
inisters to Prince Harry and Meghan Markle.
n in the UK in 1973, she grew up in the Middle East
later educated at Cambridge University and the
ropean University Institute in Florence.

Praise for

the skills

mpelling primer on how women can forge a path to
ss. The practicality and clarity of Husain's advice
a source of new strength for women in the daily
to both fulfil their potential and get their due in the
orkplace'   TINA BROWN

'I wish I'd been able to read this book when I was 20. Mind
you, it's never too late'   CLARE BALDING

'This book is a must-read for anyone (woman or man) who aspires to reach the top of their game'

'From speaking up to rising up, this book is full of practical advice for young women ready to realise their full potential'

'This is the perfect guide on how to get where you want to be' *Red*

'With the confidence and authority of a woman who has both attained her dream job and loves it, she meditates on what it took for her – and other women – to work their way there. This is not a memoir; it's more a feminist manifesto' *Daily Mail*

'This is the new go-to handbook for every working woman' *Emerald Street*

mishal husain

the skills

how to win at work

4th ESTATE • *London*

4th Estate
An imprint of HarperCollins*Publishers*
1 London Bridge Street
London SE1 9GF

www.4thEstate.co.uk

First published in Great Britain in 2018 by 4th Estate
This 4th Estate paperback edition published in 2020

1

A catalogue record for this book is
available from the British Library

ISBN 978-0-00-822066-2

Graphs on pp. 26, 46 and 215 redrawn by Martin Brown;
images on p. 143 redrawn by Joe Bright.

Printed and bound in Great Britain by
CPI Group (UK) Ltd, Croydon

MIX
Paper from
responsible sources
FSC™ C007454

This book is produced from independently certified FSC paper
to ensure responsible forest management.

For more information visit: www.harpercollins.co.uk/green

For my parents, Shama and Tazi

Contents

the skills

Introduction

Authority, purpose, confidence, looking like the person in the office who is clearly going places – if there was one thing I wanted to achieve in writing this book, it was to inject a '*how*' into statements about the workplace based around those words and ideas. How could they be translated into the day-to-day reality of an office, a job interview, a board meeting or a speaking engagement?

I wanted to use the tools of my own trade of broadcasting to answer that question, especially the pressures and perils of live work. But I was also conscious of the gulf between how people in jobs like mine are generally perceived – unencumbered by doubts about their performance – and my own experience of what it can be like in reality. I worried that when teenagers I spoke to in schools told me 'You must never get nervous', that was an assumption that might lead them to conclude that a path like mine could only be for someone blessed from birth with an unshakeable belief in their abilities.

I also knew from my own life how self-doubt can make you baulk at opportunities that – were they presented to anyone else – would be perceived as a no-brainer. When the incoming editor of the *Today* programme asked if I might be interested in becoming one of its presenters, baulk was exactly what I did. Despite nearly twenty years as a journalist, and a long-held ambition to present one of the BBC's flagship programmes, I could only think of how hard the job would be – the precision required, the pressure, the scrutiny, the pre-dawn starts. I went home and told my husband it was a nice idea but I couldn't imagine going for it. He looked incredulous. What would I say, he asked, if any of our children ducked out of a potentially great opportunity by saying it would be too hard?

I knew the answer to that one, and it pushed me to go for it. But for the first three years on *Today*, I fretted about almost every shift. I could not feel at ease in the role, always worrying about what might go wrong and agonising over everything that I did. But then came a moment of change – a point from which my experience started to feel different. Although an element of apprehension remained about what the working day would bring, that worry started to feel manageable and something I could channel. Looking back, it is easy to see that over time I grew into the role and began to feel more at home in it. Yet to me, at first that outcome was never a given. I find myself wondering now, what if I had bailed sometime before that moment of change? I'd be looking back and probably perceiving my uncertainty as evidence that the job wasn't right for me. I would never have discovered what I can now appreciate – that the passage of time, perseverance and an increasing familiarity made an immense difference.

Along the way I have learned a lot about how more difficult tasks develop your capabilities, and about scrutiny and resilience. My work is on public display, with the low points as well as the high subject to immediate and sometimes fevered comment. It is often intense, both because of unusual working hours – a regular 3 a.m. alarm call – and the pressure that comes from having to quickly absorb large quantities of information. The end result is all about conveying that information in a form that best serves the audience – getting the most salient and important facts, thoughts and opinions out of interviewees, and being as clear as possible in your own thought and speech.

However much that is at the core of my working life, I have always found it much more difficult to convey information about myself, particularly in the way that is essential in the workplace. It starts with how you present your skills and aptitude at an interview and goes on through promotions and appraisals to getting the senior-most positions. As time went on, I realised I needed to deploy the essential tools of my trade – choice of words, body language, ability to distil information and deploying facts – towards my own career development as well as on the television and radio. In an age where myriad information sources and social media mean that attention spans tend to be short, those messages about yourself need to be ever more instantly understandable and memorable.

Why did I find these conversations and messages trickier than my day-to-day work and shy away from anything that I perceived as showcasing or selling it? I had certainly grown up with a strong motivation to be the best that I possibly could be – largely stemming from being the daughter of immigrants and seeing how my parents had uprooted themselves from all that was familiar, strongly driven by wanting to do their utmost for us children. Both came to the UK from Pakistan – my father as a young doctor and my mother when she married him a few years later. There was never any question of me, as their daughter, being perceived differently from my brother; for both of us, the arrival of school reports sparked a gathering around the dining table where my father would read each entry aloud. As long as we appeared to be doing our best, he was satisfied: 'Aim high,' he would say, 'because if you miss what you are aiming for, you'll still end up in a good place.'

In both my parents' families, mine would be the third generation in which women had had educational opportunities comparable to men – back in the 1930s, in what was then British India, my two grandmothers were enrolled on medical and nursing courses respectively. In the 1980s, it was the desire for me to have the best possible education that made my parents opt for an English boarding school rather than have me stay in Saudi Arabia, where we were then living. It was a decision that meant difficult airport goodbyes and long separations. Years later, I discovered that quality of schooling was not the only factor. As a teenage girl in Saudi Arabia I would have had to wear the long black *abaya*, or cloak, and a headscarf every time I left the house. My parents worried that being subject to those constraints as part of my daily life might fundamentally alter my sense of what I could go on to achieve.

All of this support helped to propel me forward through my teenage years, but sometime during university I think I became less sure of myself and more self-conscious. I would have gained so much more from the experience of university had I been more willing to ask questions, to take risks and to test out arguments in front of my lecturers and fellow students. Instead, I was rather too cautious, apprehensive that I might have misunderstood, misjudged or appear uninformed. Something of that persisted in the first part of my professional life, when I was a producer first at Bloomberg TV and then at the BBC, before getting into presenting at the age of twenty-seven. I would mull over running orders and scripts in search of the ideal turn of phrase or link between one story and the next. I would approach new projects, such as working on the Olympics, almost like an exam – setting aside time for preparation, making extensive notes in advance and trying to cover every base. Working on *Today* knocked that search for perfection out of me for the most basic of reasons: the shortage of time focused the mind like nothing I had previously experienced, forcing me to trust my instincts and judgements and helping to give me a new-found courage.

I look back now and wish that I had kept hold of my self-belief all along the way. Instead, somewhere between entering the workplace and having to rise to the challenge of a particularly exacting role, it took a back seat. The socialisation of girls and the way they can then end up deferring to their male peers was certainly a factor, but later on it was also hard to hold on to a sense that I could make it into senior roles through the intense periods of pregnancy and early parenthood. The top of my chosen field, as in many others at that time, was one where women were under-represented, and women of colour more so.

Even today, and even in the most progressive nations, too many companies and workplaces can be gender-mapped into a pyramid shape: women and men represented in equal numbers at entry level but the presence of women tailing off dramatically the more senior the role.[1] At the beginning of 2018, just seven women were leading FTSE 100 companies, fewer than the number of men called David occupying the same positions.[2] A century after the first woman was elected to Parliament at Westminster, around two-thirds of British MPs are men,[3] with a similar picture among partners in law firms in England and Wales, where only a third are women.[4] On the airwaves, a 2018 study of the UK's six most prominent broadcast news programmes found 2.2 male experts appearing for every female one.[5] In some professions, even the entry level is seriously out of kilter – only around 12 per cent of all engineers in the UK are female.[6] After the Harvey Weinstein scandal, the actor Emma Thompson called the lack of women in the film industry a 'gender dysfunction', part of a malaise within the system. 'There are not nearly enough women, particularly in Hollywood, in positions of power. There aren't enough women at the top of the tree – in the studios – who could perhaps balance everything out. There aren't enough women on set. This is part of our difficulty.'[7]

I still find myself in settings that are overwhelmingly male, often at conferences – including the high-profile World Economic Forum, in Davos, where many of the women present are journalists or conference staff. It can be intimidating to look around the room and become conscious of being one of a small minority. Or you can see it as a galvanising moment. At Davos, I was once in an off-the-record media session with the Iranian president when, as the questions began, I debated whether I had one worthy of asking. And then I realised that as there were only about ten women in a gathering of well over a hundred people, if I didn't speak up, the session might well end without a female voice being heard at all. Suddenly, the principle of participation seemed far more important than the actual question. I stuck up my hand and spoke.

We are in a time of increased awareness about the importance of representation across so many groups, but when I hear people say confidently that their daughters won't experience the same realities and the same barriers, I am not convinced. My generation has had opportunities that most of our mothers did not, but we've also come up against obstacles that many of us expected would be gone by now. Work and childcare remain a difficult balancing act for too many women, and the bulk of home responsibilities are also mostly ours. Gender pay gaps illustrate the paucity of women in higher-paid roles, while equal pay claims raise questions about how women are perceived and valued in comparison with their male colleagues. Those gaps can be there even when women are in the most pre-eminent positions – such as Claire Foy in the lead role of Queen Elizabeth in *The Crown*, who was paid less than the male actor in the supporting role of her husband Prince Philip.

It seems to me that men set off on their careers with an expectation of advancement, unburdened by the questions or worries that can dog women – especially what may lie ahead of them in terms of juggling a career and family life. Bearing the weight of childcare responsibilities can reduce the ability to take advantage of salary-boosting job offers, because women are more tied to their commute, working hours and keeping their routine unchanged. And when they take up part-time and flexible working options the result can be a disproportionate wage penalty, a promotion penalty or simply a perception that their priorities now lie elsewhere. Ellen Kullman, who was one of the most powerful women in American business when she was running the corporate giant DuPont, has said that during her time in that company, women were being promoted every 30–36 months, while men were moving on every 18–24 months. The women seemed to be regarded as needing longer to show their capability.[8]

Perceptions can also be a barrier to women's own sense of their potential. I know that when I close my eyes and conjure up an image of someone at the top of my chosen profession – a main presenter or a prominent interviewer – I see a man. I see a white man, as it happens. This reflects the reality of the world that has surrounded me in my time in broadcasting, but there is an internal effect, too, which makes it harder to imagine yourself in those pole positions one day. Early on in my career, there were times when I felt my suggestions weren't taken as seriously as a man's might have been ('Stick to what you're good at' was one comment from a manager when I offered an opinion beyond my core brief). And even now, there are times when a prominent contributor walks into the studio and looks across at my co-presenter, and I imagine them wishing he was doing the interview with them rather than me.

It has taken me a while to feel I have a right to be in that room, in a position that allows me to question some of the most powerful people in the land. It's what I think of as the third phase of my career. During the first, when I got a foot in the door of the news industry, I felt an immense thrill – although there was also a period on overnight shifts when it was hard to feel energised about anything at all. I certainly didn't think about a future as a presenter, which was a world away from my life at that time. However, the business programme I was working on at the BBC sometimes got producers to do short on-camera wraps of the day on the financial markets. After doing this a few times I was offered some reporting shifts. Then, one week, there was a gap in the business presenters' rota and I was asked to fill in, my knees shaking under the studio desk as I did so. I never went back to being a producer and in the next few years the opportunities came thick and fast – I had a stint based in Singapore and one in Washington, by which time I was with the international channel BBC World News.

Then came what I now think of as the middle phase of my career, coinciding with an intense period in my personal life – twenty months after the birth of my first son, I had twin boys. Returning to work after my second maternity leave was all about keeping the show on the road – life needed to be as simple and manageable as possible, in order to meet the needs of the family and keep my hand in at work. As the domestic rhythm became a little more settled and just a little less intense, however, I started to wonder what the next stage of my career could involve. Radio 4 had been a companion to my life from the age of seventeen – when a wise person advised me that listening to it would be good preparation for university interviews – and I knew I would love to work there one day. But I had no experience in radio production or reporting, let alone presenting on this medium. The only way I could gain valuable experience and get my voice on air would be to use my days off to do occasional shifts, filling in on news and other factual programmes in the hope that it might stand me in good stead for any future opportunities.

None appeared to be forthcoming, though, and this was an odd and often disheartening time – making ad-hoc appearances on unfamiliar programmes, wondering if I was in danger of becoming a jack-of-all-trades. What motivated me to keep going was the strong sense that I had but one life to see how far I might progress – I didn't want to look back later and wish I had tried a bit harder. I realised, however, that the speed with which my career had taken off when I started presenting on television meant that opportunities had come my way without me having to push for them. I had got used to that, and I was now lacking an essential skill: being able to make a pitch for myself. I went to see one BBC editor after another, asking if they might try me out, but I found myself struggling with straightforward questions about what I wanted to do. In my quest not to come across as unrealistic or full of myself, I failed to have compelling answers that were true to who I was and where I wanted to go in my career.

Over time, there were some valuable lessons: I learned to hone in advance exactly how I wanted to use each meeting and be clear about what I was asking for; to be ready to turn my energies towards a new avenue if the first one didn't work out; to keep an open mind and explore multiple options, even though that sometimes felt overwhelming; to do my best to express my hopes and ambitions without apology or diffidence – even if it felt excruciating at some moments and pushy at others. From there I started to think about nurturing a set of skills that might be relevant to career troughs as well as peaks, adaptable to different settings and transferable even in the event of a complete career change. Every projection about the future of work suggests that mobility will be increasingly important – perhaps the disruption will even bridge some of the workplace gender gaps we see today, if it becomes more common for men *and* women to shift gear, go part-time or take time out for family reasons.

Today, when I contrast my experience of working life with that of my mother, I feel a deep gratitude. For all the emphasis on education in my family, the idea that it could be used to forge a career and for that career to exist alongside motherhood, is a novel one. My mother gained two degrees in Pakistan and became a producer at Pakistan Television when it was first set up in the 1960s. But all around her it was accepted that marriage and motherhood were more than likely to bring a career to an end. After her marriage brought her to the UK in 1972, I was born in 1973 and became her full-time job. She told me years later that there were times when she would watch the Asian programming coming out of the BBC in Birmingham and long to be a part of it, to use her experience and have an identity in this new country beyond that of wife and mother. It was never going to be possible; my father was working long hours as an NHS doctor in Northamptonshire and Bedfordshire and any family members who might have helped out were far away. Childcare and travel costs would have been an unjustifiable addition to an already tight household budget.

It is not in my mother's nature to be bitter about what might have been, but her experience reminds me not to lose an appreciation of the doors that have been open to me, one generation on. Changed attitudes to women and to ethnic minorities have both played a key role in my life chances – not so long ago it would have been hard to imagine someone with a name like mine fronting a national news programme. That is not to say that I find my own combination of motherhood, marriage and work easy – or even always manageable. I often think back to what I heard the then head coach of UK Athletics, Charles van Commenee, say just ahead of the London Olympics. Having coached many athletes to medals, he said he always tried to make them appreciate that pressure would be an ongoing part of their lives. 'I tell them – it's uncomfortable out there,' he said. The words resonate with me because alongside the many privileges of my job are the difficult aspects – in particular the scrutiny. I cannot have one without accepting the other, and I have but this one life to make the most of what comes my way.

Where We Are

Each generation must create its own reality and find its own identity

Camille Paglia

If I feel fortunate to have been born in a time when my opportunities have been so much greater than my mother's, it is also true that the advancement of women has not reached the point I would have imagined it might when I left university in 1995. By then, both the UK and my parents' country of origin, Pakistan, had elected female prime ministers and, if asked, I would have said that spoke volumes about change and progress.

More than twenty years on, I now see that while we owe a great deal to those who smashed glass ceilings and led the way, the follow-up – assuming there is one – is vital. It was Norway's Erna Solberg, the second woman to be elected prime minister of her country, who brought this home when she told me why she likes the 'second woman' tag: 'It means the first was not a one-off'. Even her country, known for being one of the most gender-equal in the world, has not reached a fifty-fifty split in Parliament

– although with 41 per cent women, it is still doing better than most.[1] In India, women make up only 12 per cent of the Lok Sabha, or lower house of Parliament, while in China a woman has never sat on the Communist Party's most powerful decision-making body, the Politburo Standing Committee.[2]

Interestingly, the picture for Chinese business is considerably better, with women holding 31 per cent of senior leadership roles. It's a proportion matched in Africa and exceeded in Eastern Europe, but higher than businesses in the European Union (27 per cent) and in North America (21 per cent).[3] Notably, the study by Grant Thornton International found that those countries with the most policies in place to promote equality – equal pay, parental leave, flexible working – were not necessarily those with the greatest diversity at the top of business. Policy alone was not producing large scale change, they said, while stereotypes about gender roles were still a barrier to progress. That is a conclusion that perhaps makes clearer where the focus for my generation and younger women should lie – we need to think about individuals as well as institutions.

We can take heart, however, from studies that have compared companies' records on diversity and their performance – one analysis of more than 20,000 firms in 91 countries found that the presence of women in corporate leadership correlated positively with profitability.[4] Another, from consultants at McKinsey, reported that a correlation between gender and ethnic diversity and financial performance generally holds true across geographies. While they couldn't say that one *caused* the other, they observed a 'real relationship between diversity and performance' and said the reasons for it would include 'improved access to talent, enhanced decision making and depth of consumer insight and strengthened employee engagement and licence to operate'.[5]

A broad perspective on where there's been progress – and where there are gaps – comes from the World Economic Forum's annual analysis of gender-based disparities. In recent years it has found that the countries studied had made great strides in two key areas – health and educational attainment. The major gaps lay in two others – political empowerment and economic participation and opportunity.[6] Its reports have also highlighted how women are likely to be affected by key future trends: automation will significantly affect industries in which many are currently employed, and they are under-represented in high-income and high-growth fields such as technology and science. Even countries where women have made great strides cannot be assured of future progress, explains the organisation's head of education, gender and work, Saadia Zahidi: 'A lot of advanced economies have stalled as they were riding the wave of the education boom among women, but if the responsibility of home and childcare is still on those women, there is a limit to how much they can do in the workplace.'[7]

India is a country where the growth in girls' education hasn't resulted in women entering the workforce in the numbers you might expect or hope for. In fact, according to the Harvard economist Professor Rohini Pande, female participation in the Indian labour market fell between 1990 and 2015, down from 37 per cent to 28 per cent. It's not a lack of political will to get more women into paid employment, she says, or a lack of interest from women themselves. Instead, there is a significant role being played by social norms – among parents, husbands and parents-in-law – about appropriate behaviour for women. Pande's research also suggests that while low pay is the main reason for Indian men to leave a job or not accept one, women cite family pressures and responsibilities.[8]

Those pressures might relate to taking care of the household, but also basic mobility, such as requiring permission to go out. As Professor Pande says: 'It's pretty difficult to look for a job if you can't leave the house alone.' Even in India's urban areas, she and her associate Charity Troyer Moore found female workers struggling to access male-dominated networks. 'Women often end up in lower-paid and less-responsible positions than their abilities would otherwise allow,' they say, 'which, in turn, makes it less likely that they will choose to work at all, especially as household incomes rise and they don't absolutely have to work to survive.'[9]

Nonetheless, the experience of a country like Bangladesh, with similar social and cultural norms to India, shows that there are ways such barriers *can* be tackled. It has a higher proportion of working women than India, largely thanks to the development of its garment industry, where 80 per cent of the workers are female. On a trip there in 2015, I saw for myself the difference that a job in one of these factories can make to an individual's life. In a room packed with rows of women at sewing machines, one young worker's ID card, hanging around her neck, bore the photograph of a young boy on the reverse. She was a widow and this was her only child. His future was her biggest motivation and she was able to pay for his education thanks to her job – without it, they would both be dependent on the mercy of relatives. Indeed, Pande and Moore say the garment sector has been important for Bangladeshi women's empowerment far beyond the factory floor: 'The explosive growth of that industry during the last thirty years caused a surge in large-scale female labour force participation. It also delayed marriage age and caused parents to invest more in their daughters' education.'[10]

In the UK much of the conversation about workplace gaps between men and women has focused on pay, especially after a 2017 law required larger employers to reveal the difference in the mean and median pay of male and female workers. As this gender pay reporting is based on averages it is in some ways a crude calculation – the airline easyJet, for example, reported a particularly large gap because men dominate its cohort of pilots, who are paid considerably more than the mostly female cabin crew.

It does, however, shine a light on representation and getting women into higher-paid roles, which is why Carolyn Fairbairn of the Confederation of British Industry welcomes it: 'This is about fairness but it's also about productivity in our economy and how we have businesses that have all the talents. We do not have enough women who are pilots, or CEOs who are women, or enough top senior consultants in hospitals who are women. These are issues that we now need to really grip.'[11] Some believe the obligation to report has transformed companies' conversations about gender. 'When we've talked about the pay gap before, the response has always been "That must be happening somewhere else", says Ann Francke of the Chartered Management Institute. Now, she says companies are being forced to confront their data and reflect on the picture it paints.[12]

Elsewhere, other data allows comparisons of pay for men and women who have the same professional occupation. A 2017 data set from the UK's Office for National Statistics showed considerable gender variation in average hourly earnings in many of them. Among full-time financial managers and directors, for example, men earned an average of £35.52 per hour (or £72,000 per year), and women £24.29 per hour, translating into an annual salary of around £43,000. The pattern was similar for town planning officers, musicians, scientists and chief executives. Most of the roles where the gap disappeared or was reversed, so that women were earning more (secretaries and fitness instructors, for example), had hourly earnings at the lower end of the spectrum.[13]

It is possible that these comparisons mask variations about the work done within the different categories: the scope and responsibility of the roles, whether the jobs were in the public or private sector, the region in which they were based and the skills, experience and competence of the individuals whose information went into the data set. But like companies' gender pay gap figures, they can be a valuable starting point for a conversation about disparities. Perhaps the women had previously taken time out from work or been part-time for a period – but would that, or should that, fully account for the gap with comparable men once they returned to full-time?

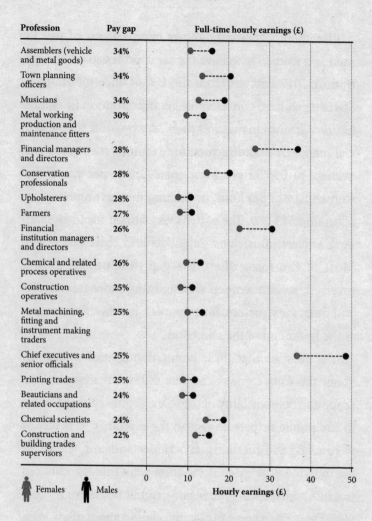

Profession	Pay gap	Full-time hourly earnings (£)
Assemblers (vehicle and metal goods)	34%	
Town planning officers	34%	
Musicians	34%	
Metal working production and maintenance fitters	30%	
Financial managers and directors	28%	
Conservation professionals	28%	
Upholsterers	28%	
Farmers	27%	
Financial institution managers and directors	26%	
Chemical and related process operatives	26%	
Construction operatives	25%	
Metal machining, fitting and instrument making traders	25%	
Chief executives and senior officials	25%	
Printing trades	25%	
Beauticians and related occupations	24%	
Chemical scientists	24%	
Construction and building trades supervisors	22%	

Females Males

Hourly earnings (£)

From the ONS Annual Survey of Hours and Earnings 2017

According to the Institute for Fiscal Studies, part-time work can have a striking effect in shutting down normal wage progression. In general, pay rises with experience, but part-time workers, who are mostly women, miss out on these gains. 'By the time a first child is grown up (aged twenty), mothers earn about 30 per cent less per hour, on average, than similarly educated fathers. About a quarter of that wage gap is explained by the higher propensity of the mothers to have been in part-time rather than full-time paid work while that child was growing up, and the consequent lack of wage progression,' said the 2019 study, highlighting what the authors called 'the long-term depressing effect' of part-time work.[14]

At Harvard, the economist Professor Claudia Goldin has examined the way different jobs are structured in order to see how this sort of pay penalty might be addressed. She's pointed to how some occupations – including within business, finance and the law – generally pay a premium for longer hours. A lawyer expected to be readily available for clients and working sixty hours per week, for example, is likely to earn more than double the salary of a comparable colleague working thirty hours a week. Professor Goldin says this 'non-linearity' arises when the job is set up or has historically been done in a way that makes it difficult for workers to substitute for one another. Within this environment, those who work shorter hours will suffer a disproportionate wage penalty.

She contrasts that with what has happened in the United States with pharmacists, a high-income profession in which women are well represented. In the 1970s the sector was dominated by small independent businesses, with many self-employed pharmacists, but today the majority are employees of large companies or hospitals. Part-time working is common, but pay tends to be perfectly in line with the number of hours worked – those who do fewer hours are paid proportionately less. Goldin attributes this to the ease with which pharmacists are able to substitute for one another – no single person is required to be available for an extended number of hours or for certain hours of the day. 'The spread of vast information systems and the standardisation of drugs have enhanced their ability to seamlessly hand off clients and be good substitutes for one another. The result is that short and irregular hours are not penalised.'[15]

Professor Goldin says this structure helps to make it worthwhile for women to stay in paid work rather than leave to care for families, and that other professions could learn from the example of pharmacy. There will still be roles where employees won't easily be able to swap in for each other – the founder of a business perhaps, or someone with unique and non-replicable expertise – but these should be fewer than is the case at present.

Sometimes internal reward systems are worth re-evaluating, especially if they have been in place for years. When a BBC investigation showed that 95 out of the

100 highest-paid hospital consultants in England were male, bonuses for clinical excellence, accumulating over time, turned out to be a considerable factor.[16] One consultant, Mahnaz Hashmi, told me what applying for the bonuses involves: 'You have to fill out a lengthy form within a short time-frame of a few weeks, showcasing your achievements and providing evidence for them. If you are part-time you will have less to put down. In the early stages it feels like a lot of effort for relatively small bonuses, but they become more valuable as they accumulate over the years.'

This NHS process was based around consultants putting themselves forward. 'Women seem to do this less,' she says. It also demanded a lot of the doctor's own time – for example serving on awards committees, thereby making sure they were up to date with the latest criteria and scoring. 'It's difficult to do when you are part-time, and if you come back to full-time you usually find there's already a wide salary differential between men and women consultants.' My BBC colleague Nick Triggle says he was struck when working on the data by the self-perpetuating nature of the system. 'Those working in the NHS told me younger consultants often only go for the awards after prompting from older ones, and there was a sense that senior figures are more likely to do this for those who remind them of their younger selves,' he says. 'The culture created, perhaps unconsciously, is one where men encourage other men towards the pay awards.'

In the summer of 2017, my own workplace was the setting for what turned out to be a lengthy row sparked by the BBC disclosing the salaries of the highest-earning on-air 'talent' – including presenters, contributors and actors – paid directly from the licence fee.[17] The list, which included me, generated intense interest and comment: few people from ethnic minorities were among the ninety-six names, while people who went to private schools were over-represented, compared to the population as a whole.[18] Most of the scrutiny, however, was focused on gender – the top seven earners were all male, and in some cases, there was a marked difference between the salaries of women and men appearing on the same programmes. The leading businessman Sir Philip Hampton, chairman of the drugs giant GSK, wondered why women broadcasters had let it happen. 'How has this arisen at the BBC that these intelligent, high-powered, sometimes formidable women have sat in this situation?'[19]

The answer is that we didn't know what the situation was until the disclosure. It sparked unprecedented conversations between colleagues, with women and men starting to share information about their salaries and, in some cases, their efforts to be paid equally to their peers. Some were in pay brackets that put them above the national average, others were not. And we wondered: if the system wasn't treating women with agency and clout equally to men, what did that say about what might be happening to women elsewhere?

It's happened even in companies which were sure their ethos would have guarded against any question of unequal pay. In 2015, the chief executive of the tech company Salesforce, Marc Benioff, was approached by his human resources chief about conducting an equal pay audit for its thirty thousand employees. Benioff thought it unnecessary, telling CBS News later that his company had a great culture: 'We don't play shenanigans paying people unequally. It's unheard of.' Yet he agreed to the audit, which went on to reveal not a few isolated cases but a persistent pay gap between men and women doing the same job. 'It was through the whole company,' said Benioff. 'Every division, every department, every geography.' Salesforce ended up giving 10 per cent of its female employees pay rises, but when it conducted another audit, the results showed that further adjustments were needed. 'It turned out we had bought about two dozen companies. And guess what? When you buy a company you also buy its pay practices.' Benioff concluded that there was a much bigger issue afoot. 'I think it's happening everywhere. There's a cultural phenomenon where women are paid less.'[20]

Not everyone agrees with that, instead emphasising choice and its implications – for example, women deciding against pursuing time-intensive but financially rewarding career paths.[21] But in Iceland, the government is placing a legal obligation on any employer of more than twenty-five people to undertake a similar exercise to Salesforce's – a comprehensive assessment allowing them to be certified as paying equal wages for work of equal value. The process requires individual jobs to be analysed and scored against a list of criteria, including education required, level of responsibility, how demanding the role is and its value to the employer. The scores across the company or organisation are then compared and any gap between two jobs with the same score but different pay must be addressed. When Iceland's Directorate of Customs piloted the system, the results included the role of statistics analyst being judged equal to that of a legal adviser, which had previously been higher paid. The statistics analysts were given a rise. The head of human resources, Unnur Kristjánsdóttir, said there was a wider dividend too: 'We have a happier workforce, knowing that the salary system is something they can trust.'[22]

The new focus on gender is adding an urgency to questions being asked in many different settings including at two of the world's top universities. Both Oxford and Cambridge have been puzzling over a gender gap at the highest levels of attainment – first-class degrees in some subjects. In 2014, Cambridge's results in history showed that in the first part of the degree course, 88 per cent of the firsts went to male students, despite there being near equal numbers of men and women enrolled.[23] At Oxford that year, 35 per cent of men but only 21 per cent of women studying English gained a first-class degree and there has been a persistent gender attainment gap in chemistry, too.[24]

At both universities, all students would have entered with excellent exam grades, and the effort to understand the gaps is made more complex by the range of subjects involved: from the essay-based humanities, where marking is more subjective, to the exactitude required in the sciences. At Oxford, Pro-Vice-Chancellor and Advocate for Diversity Rebecca Surender told me they have been looking at everything from pre-university education to the admissions process, exposure to female role models and the style of teaching, for example the often intense interaction in weekly tutorials. 'The kind of degree you get matters and we don't want women to be disadvantaged when they leave us and go into the world,' she says. 'Preliminary results suggest that there is no single explanation but rather a set of interactions between wider socialisation and what happens before women get to us, together with some environmental factors in the institution.'

At Cambridge one study investigated the relationship between exam structure and performance. Academics in the physics department set up a mock exam for first-year undergraduates in which, for some questions, the usual format was replaced with a 'scaffolded' version, broken down into sections showing the marks available for each.[25] This style is closer to what those undergraduates would have been accustomed to in their school-leaving exams, and while it resulted in improved performance for all candidates, the women benefited more than the men. On average their marks increased by more than 13 per cent compared with their previous exam performance – while for the men the average increase was 9 per cent.

Dame Athene Donald, one of Cambridge's most senior female professors and a physicist herself, told me a close focus on the beginning of the university experience was vital: 'If women come here and struggle in their first year, they may never gain the confidence to proceed. In a subject like physics, where the percentage of girls is only 20–25, and you will be conscious at some level of being in a minority, it can feel even more threatening. Sometimes young women don't like to say "I'm struggling" because they think that's an admission of failure, so they struggle in silence.'

She wonders about the impact of stereotypes – perhaps young women don't *expect* to do well in a mathematics-heavy subject such as physics – but also why more progress hasn't been made since her own days as an undergraduate at the university. 'In my final year class there were eight women out of about 100. But one didn't expect anything else. I knew perfectly well that there were only three colleges that could admit women. What I find shocking today is that despite all the changes, despite the fact that we are fully co-educational apart from three women's colleges, we still have these issues.'

At Oxford, one of the studies overseen by Rebecca Surender has focused on academic self-concept, or the belief in your ability to succeed in a particular subject area. Given that this tends to correlate with academic achievement, the aim was to establish any differences between men and women on arrival at the university and how their academic self-concept might change during the first year of study. She told me the findings showed that from the beginning of their course, male students had a higher perception of their own competence in their subject compared with their female peers, but for both sexes the level remained stable over the course of the academic year.

For the university this is of course a welcome finding because it suggests that the difference exists before students arrive. I do wonder, however, if there might also be an impact from the history, tradition and sense of excellence honed over centuries that surrounds you in these environments. I certainly remember times when I found Cambridge intimidating. The *Times* journalist Sathnam Sanghera, who was born into a working-class Sikh family and went on to read English at Cambridge, remembers 'negative feelings of unbelonging' while he was there.[26] If academic self-concept is the key, how much might it be affected in people who have a nagging sense that they don't quite fit or fully deserve to be in such a celebrated place?

In one study, researchers used a different university environment to investigate how peer perception and gender might influence students' assessments of each other. Sarah Eddy and Daniel Grunspan asked biology undergraduates to complete surveys, getting them to high-light peers they felt were particularly strong in their grasp of the material studied and those they thought would do well on the course.

The results showed that male students were much more likely to rate other men as knowledgeable, a tendency that lasted throughout the academic year and persisted even after controlling for class performance and outspokenness. Female students showed no gender bias, nominating both fellow female and male students. The authors also found that there were some students who stood out in the eyes of their peers and were nominated multiple times, and that these students were always male. It wasn't as though there weren't women with similarly high grades in their classes, who also spoke up frequently and demonstrated their knowledge, but somehow they never gained the same 'celebrity status' as their male counterparts.[27]

When I read this study I started to imagine what the scene in the classroom might have looked like. The 'celebrity' students would no doubt have been aware of attracting their peers' attention when they spoke – heads would have turned to listen to them, perhaps nodding in agreement. It's a good experience to have, one that's certain to make you feel more at ease, happier with your command of the subject material and probably spurred on to make further points. Could these apparently small interactions build up and develop capacity in a subject so much so that attainment is higher – or the chances of further study or a career in the field are increased? I started to think more and more about expectations of behaviour – whether in a classroom, smaller tutorial-style gatherings of students, or the first day in a new job. If we grow up with assumptions, even ones of which we are barely conscious, that men will speak first or take the lead, that can easily turn into a pattern that validates and reinforces those assumptions.

Consider this alongside evidence on discrimination within the workplace or before people even get there.

One meta-analysis of studies conducted in OECD countries over a twenty-five-year period found that discrimination against ethnic minority applicants in the hiring process was commonplace.[28] In 2009, research commissioned by the UK government reported high levels of name-based discrimination when researchers sent out multiple applications for real-life openings. The main difference between the applications was the likely ethnicity associated with their name: 'Andrew Clarke' was used to denote a white British male; 'Mariam Namagembe' for a black African female and 'Nazia Mahmood' for a Pakistani or Bangladeshi female. White names were favoured over equivalent applications from ethnic minority candidates.[29]

More recently, big data analayses have been used to look at information about individuals in new ways. The US-based neuroscientist and artificial intelligence expert Vivienne Ming took a vast data set of millions of real-life professional profiles collected by a tech recruitment firm and used them to compare the career trajectories of software developers whose first names were either 'Joe' or 'Jose'. She found that those named 'Jose' typically needed a Master's degree or more to be equally likely to get a promotion as a 'Joe' who had no degree. She called this a 'tax on being different', because of the extra costs and time involved in gaining the higher qualifications.

When Ming then used her model to compare the profiles of software engineers with male names against those with female names, she also found a 'tax'. Typically, women needed a Master's degree in order to compete with a man with a Bachelor's degree. No wonder people who face these extra hurdles sometimes decide it's not worth pursuing a particular path, she concluded: 'The tax comes from the cost of studying at more prestigious universities, on more and higher degrees, in increases in minimum experience, and more exceptional professional backgrounds.' In the face of this, any decision to drop out is rational, reflecting 'a cost almost entirely absent from their more privileged peers'.[30]

Having invested in recruitment and development, few companies or organisations would want to see good staff reach a conclusion like that, disappearing from career tracks they had embarked upon. When that happens, both the individual and the employer generally lose out, with evidence of wider economic impact too. Yet without a forensic approach to achieving progress and change, where we are now could easily be where we stall.

Instead, we need to be laser-like about identifying where the pressure points arise and why. What is it that deters or derails people with potential, who have much to give, and what might just keep them in the game or at least reaching the next milestone? Data and new analytical tools should help provide evidence and illustrate patterns, but it is only that degree of clear-sighted focus that will lead to better solutions for the twenty-first-century workplace.

Growing Up Female

We say to girls, you can have ambition,
but not too much. You should aim to be
successful, but not too successful

Chimamanda Ngozi Adichie

What do we see and hear, growing up as girls, that might have a lasting impact on our sense of self? As a child I remember often being asked what I wanted to become, but a few years ago I started to guard against something that I realised was creeping into my own conversations with the young daughters of friends. Too often, I might include a comment on their appearance – something that seemed innocuous enough at the time but was also unlikely to be said to boys. It started to bother me. If it would be odd for my sons' hair or clothes to be the source of comment when they were introduced to another adult, why was I doing that when it came to their female peers?

We send messages about behaviour, too – expecting girls to be polite and well-behaved while making a fuss of boys when they are. And girls notice. Girlguiding UK, which carries out an annual survey of opinion among nearly two thousand girls and young women, has raised the alarm over the entrenchment of gender stereotypes: 'From a young age, girls sense they face different expectations compared to boys and feel a pressure to adjust their behaviour accordingly. Girls encounter stereotyping across their lives – at school, in the media and in advertising, in the real and the virtual world, from their peers, teachers and families.' Among the seven- to ten-year-olds questioned more than half said gender stereotypes would affect them saying what they thought and how much they participated in class.[1]

One group of US researchers has suggested that six is a key age at which impressions about the different potential of boys and girls start to set in. In their study, groups of children were told a story about someone described as 'really, really smart', i.e. clever, and were then shown pictures of two men and two women. They were asked to guess who the story they heard was about. Among five-year-olds, boys were most likely to pick men and girls women. But when the same process was repeated on six- and seven-year-olds, the girls in that age group were less likely than the boys to associate brilliance with their own gender. The boys hadn't changed their tendency to prefer men.

The same researchers then focused on the way two games were described to six- and seven-year-olds and how that might affect their interest. One game was said to be for 'children who are really, really smart' and the other for 'children who try really, really hard'. When the children were then asked about which game they wanted to play, girls were less likely than boys to express an interest in the one said to be for the 'really, really smart'. The authors said their work provided preliminary evidence of how gendered beliefs about intelligence develop and how they relate to young children's decision-making.[2]

If this sort of perception takes hold so young, how much might it then be exacerbated by words we use differently for boys and girls and men and women? 'Ambitious' is usually seen as a positive if you're male, much less so if you're female. 'Pushy' is similarly negative for women, but tolerable in a man, an indication that he is going places. And then there are the flattering ways to convey respect and professional standing – by referring to someone as 'distinguished' or 'esteemed' – that are very rarely used for women.

In a striking visualisation, Professor Ben Schmidt of Northeastern University illustrated this in a study based on student feedback placed on the website RateMyProfessors.com. It revealed that words such as 'genius' and 'brilliant' were more likely to be used to describe male academics.[3] Women, on the other hand, were more likely to be called 'nice' and, in general, described in terms that related to personality, attitude and behaviour ('helpful' or 'friendly'), rather than purely to their academic or intellectual capability. 'When we use these reviews and evaluations to assess people,' says Professor Schmidt, 'we need to keep in mind that the way people write them is really culturally conditioned.'[4]

Often, details about women's appearance and private lives creep into discussions that are supposedly about their

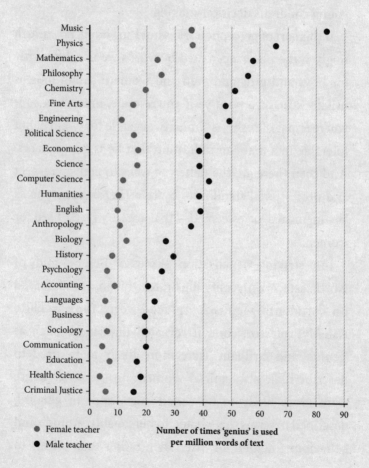

- Female teacher
- Male teacher

Number of times 'genius' is used per million words of text

professional abilities. Hillary Clinton once said that if she wanted to knock a story off the front page, all she needed to do was change her hairstyle, but it can get much more personal. Within hours of thirty-seven-year-old Jacinda Ardern becoming leader of New Zealand's Labour Party she was asked in an interview whether she had made a choice between having a career or having babies. Sometimes, women's achievements are described with references to their personal lives that would jump out as ludicrous if used for a man: when the businesswoman Rona Fairhead emerged as the preferred candidate to chair the then BBC Trust, one newspaper headline read: 'Mother of Three Poised to Lead the BBC.'

Once you focus on the imagery we consume from an early age, other oddities become apparent. That was the experience of the Oscar-winning actress Geena Davis after she started to watch children's television and films with her young daughter. 'I immediately noticed that there seemed to be far more male characters than female characters,' she later said. 'This made no sense: why on earth in the twenty-first century would we be showing fictitious worlds bereft of female characters to our children?'[5] Deciding that she needed data to convince executives that there was a problem, she founded the Geena Davis Institute on Gender in Media in 2004. Its studies have shown that even among animated family films, a ratio of three male speaking characters for every female one prevails and that two types of female characters tend to dominate: the traditional and the 'hypersexual'. These girls and women might be unusually thin and in sexually revealing clothing, or in animated films they might be depicted with an unnatural body shape, such as an exaggeratedly tiny waist.[6]

Earlier on, the cartoonist Alison Bechdel had drawn attention to the portrayal of women in film in her own way, with a 1985 strip in which two women discuss going to the cinema. One has a rule – she'll only go to see a film with at least two women in it, who talk to each other about something other than a man.[7] It sounds basic, but once you start applying what's come to be called 'the Bechdel Test', it is remarkable how few films pass it – only half of those that have ever won the Best Picture Oscar, according to a 2018 BBC analysis, and even then some of those had just one or two instances of conversation that met the requirements.[8]

Even where a film is based around a strong female protagonist, she may be outnumbered in terms of her lines. In a study of film dialogue, the data website The Pudding found that was the case in *Mulan*, where the eponymous heroine's dragon has considerably more lines than she does. Overall, male characters dominated the dialogue in 73 per cent of Disney/Pixar films analysed, including family favourites such as *Toy Story*, *The Lion*

King, Monsters, Inc. and *The Jungle Book*.[9] And a study made of films across the world found that women not only have fewer speaking roles than men, but that their characters are less likely to be portrayed having an occupation than women in the real-life workforce of those countries.[10]

Thanks to sustained and detailed work by Dr Martha M. Lauzen at San Diego State University, we also know that there has been little change in the presence of women working behind the scenes in the film industry. Her data shows that the number employed as directors, writers, producers, cinematographers and editors hasn't really budged in twenty years: today, just 11 per cent of directors and 4 per cent of cinematographers are women.[11]

Where films do have at least one female director, there is a greater likelihood of other women being employed – a correlation that makes all the difference to someone like Lucinda Coxon, who wrote the 2015 film *The Danish Girl*, and who needs to find enough work to sustain her livelihood. 'Directors are really the top of the creative tree in film,' she says, 'and the presence or absence of women in that role has a serious knock-on effect.'[12]

Thanks to the Harvey Weinstein allegations, the entire industry is under a new degree of scrutiny. Melissa Silverstein, founder of the pressure group Women and Hollywood, says it is rife with 'toxic masculinity'. 'This is an industry that is run by men and for men,' she says. 'The movies we see have mostly male leads. The women depicted are mostly young, scantily clad and have little agency – all too often they are glorified props.'[13]

One of Weinstein's own accusers painted a chilling picture of how women are widely perceived and used. 'In this industry, there are directors who abuse their position. They are very influential, that's how they can do that,' wrote Léa Seydoux. 'Another director I worked with would film very long sex scenes that lasted days. He kept watching us, replaying the scenes over and over again in a kind of stupor. It was very gross. If you're a woman working in the film industry, you have to fight because it is a very misogynistic world. Why else are salaries so unequal? Why do men earn more than women? There is no reason for it to be that way.'[14]

Lucinda Coxon believes that everyone consuming the output of this industry, one with the power to tell stories that engage and influence us, should think about the implications of its make-up: 'The vast, vast majority of dramatic product that you, your friends, family and co-workers have access to, in the cinema or on DVD, Netflix or plain old telly has been shaped by – and often exclusively shaped by – men. And that results in some serious distortions.' She points to her experience on a BAFTA jury one year, where she watched thirteen hours of prime-time British TV drama and saw female characters brutally attacked again and again, to the point where it was barely noticeable any more. 'We need to start noticing again. We need to consider how little we learn and what a warped perspective we get on the world when the gender imbalance driving its description is so strong.'

Reese Witherspoon thinks you can often see the effect of the imbalance in the lines assigned to female characters. 'I dread reading scripts that have no women involved in their creation,' she said in 2015. 'Because inevitably, the girl turns to the guy and says, "What do we do now?"' She has a point – it's happened in films from *Gone With the Wind* to *Toy Story* to Judi Dench as 'M', speaking to James Bond.[15] Perhaps it is to make women more likeable, something the screenwriter Cami Delavigne says she is often asked to do in the creative process. 'It is not "likeable" for a woman to say "No", to say "You can't do that"', she says. 'That is not charming. That is not sweet.'[16]

When you grow up female all of this surrounds you, but the mirror image is the effect of gendered beliefs and expectations on boys. 'We stifle the humanity of boys,' said the writer Chimamanda Ngozi Adichie in a 2012 speech which was later sampled by Beyoncé and distributed to every school in Sweden. 'Masculinity becomes this hard, small cage and we put boys inside the cage. We teach boys to be afraid of fear. We teach boys to be afraid of weakness, of vulnerability.' For girls, the parameters are different: 'Because I am female, I am expected to aspire to marriage,' she said. 'I am expected to make my life choices always keeping in mind that marriage is the most important. Now marriage can be a good thing, it can be a source of joy and love and mutual support. But why do we teach girls to aspire to marriage and not teach boys the same?'[17]

I see this overemphasis on marriage frequently among those with a similar south Asian heritage to my own, where women can be perceived as deficient because their private lives are not in line with societal expectations. In Pakistan, there is even evidence to suggest that some young women pursue advanced qualifications, such as medicine, more as a route towards a better marriage than a professional future. 'It is much easier for girls to get married once they are doctors and many don't really intend to work,' said one medical school vice-chancellor, Dr Javed Akram. 'I know of hundreds and hundreds of female students who have qualified as a doctor or a dentist but they have never touched a patient.'

Today, while 70 per cent of Pakistani medical students are women, they make up less than a quarter of registered doctors. The barriers range from families frowning on daughters-in-law going out to work, to the practical – childcare, transport and security.[18]

In the West, too, there are generational shifts in women's expectations. Gail Rebuck, the publishing executive whose company was behind Sheryl Sandberg's *Lean In*, contrasts her experience with that of her mother. 'For my generation it was all about escaping from our mothers' shattered dreams,' she says. 'Most of them were products of the 1950s, intelligent women and absolutely capable, but the mores of the day dictated that as soon as they got married they would be at home bringing up the family. We grew up with that sense of unfulfilled possibility, almost a silent rage.'

Gail herself was born in 1952 and started her career in the 1970s, taking charge of a major publishing house in 1991. 'When I was coming through I could only do my best and it certainly wasn't perfect in many ways,' she says. After publishing *Lean In*, she observed something different among a younger generation – a sense of 'necessary excellence' and a feeling that they needed to be the perfect executive *and* perfect mother. 'Today's forty-somethings are often angst-ridden, partially empowered but conflicted because of the equal impetus coming from this notion of excellence.'

How true this rang for me, both in terms of the age group and the feelings. I had grown up with a stay-at-home mother but found myself making my way in the world with a different set of circumstances – wonderful opportunities and possibilities, but also being pulled in disparate directions. I could not fully model myself on the example of motherhood that I had experienced as a child and concepts of excellence, perfection or guilt were more likely to hinder than help.

Where women and girls feel daunted by barriers, real or perceived, openness can be a powerful tool. In a 2013 study, researchers in the United States set out to test several theories on interventions that might encourage girls to consider careers in the physical sciences. They looked at single-sex education, exposure to a female physics teacher, bringing female scientists in to the school as speakers and class discussions on both the work of women scientists and the lack of women working in the field. That final intervention was the only one found by the researchers to have a significant positive effect. 'Explicit personal discussions regarding issues that women face in pursuing the physical sciences may help female students realize that feelings of inadequacy or discomfort they might have stem from external norms and pressures rather than from their capabilities, interests, or values,' they said.[19]

In other words, we need to talk about this, and we need to do so in a way that is not hinged on celebrating a few particularly successful women who then appear exceptional, or 'superwomen'. When Helen Fraser was leading a network of girls' schools she spoke about the pressures she witnessed, first on girls to have the perfect appearance, school record and friendships, and then 'on young women in their twenties, who as they start to build a career, form a relationship and find a place to live, are told that they need to start having children fast, or their fertility will be gone'. Against that backdrop, she worried about the impact of an 'inner critic', holding girls and women back if they thought that what they had to say wasn't good enough, interesting enough or valuable enough. 'If the female half of the population are routinely censoring themselves,' she said, 'their great ideas aren't getting aired or implemented and the world is a poorer place.'[20]

I think back to my own childhood and the frequent question 'What do you want to be when you grow up?' and wonder if, today, a better question to a girl might be 'What is your *ambition* for when you grow up?' It stakes a claim to a word so often used negatively for women. With only sons of my own, I have no real-world experience of looking close up at girls as well as boys at the age when the effect of stereotyping sets in. But in my sons I see a self-belief that I don't remember experiencing at a comparable age. Moments after one first managed to ride a bike on his own for a few wobbly metres, he asked if he might do the Tour de France one day; another, on being told that Sadiq Khan, also from a British Pakistani background, had been elected mayor of London, said: 'I think I'll go for prime minister.' Without really knowing the word ambition, they appeared to set their sights high as a matter of course. Life will teach them in time what else is required, but it's not a bad base from which to set out.

the
skills

Planning

---

*Progress depends on the choices
we make today for tomorrow*

Hillary Clinton

How should we think about the arc of our individual working lives in an age when two key challenges are disrupting them? One is the reality of longer life spans, the other the impact of technology on jobs and livelihoods as we know them today.[1] We can't at this stage know precisely how a field we are interested in or have already chosen will be affected, but we will need to think in terms of both short- and longer-term horizons. It means having a purpose with what you are doing now *and* laying the groundwork for your next role or one you hope for further down the line.

For me, the most useful approach has been to think in terms of five-year plans – five years being a period of time that is reasonably foreseeable. Not long after I started on *Today*, I mentioned my five-year approach in an interview, only to realise that, with echoes of the Soviet Union's economic plans, it probably had a slightly sinister ring to it. To me, it meant thinking about the possibilities of the future in manageable chunks of time.

When I first joined the BBC it was also a way to map some sort of route through what felt then like quite an overwhelming place. I knew people around me were doing compelling work that I could see and hear on air, but I also knew I might never be a part of it if I didn't figure out how to find my way around in a bigger sense than not getting lost in Television Centre.

For Professor Heather McGregor – who ran a firm of executive headhunters, became the *Financial Times*'s 'Mrs Moneypenny' columnist and is now dean of a business school – longer parameters are more valuable, especially at the starting point of a career. She advocates putting a ten-year plan down on paper, including the position you'd like to be in at the end of that time but also planning for an alternative result: 'Write down the reasons it might not happen. Then work out how to deal with them. As a pilot, when you plan a flight to somewhere, you always have to name an alternative airport, in case, for whatever reason, you can't land at your intended destination. Think about your career like that.'[2]

What you write down might be job-specific – a particular role, level of pay, or title – or broader, such as running your own business or working in a smaller company. After that, she says, you need to work out the barriers to getting there. 'Quite often the barriers are financial. People get stuck in jobs and careers they don't enjoy because they need to pay the rent or the mortgage. Sometimes you need to take risks to really change the direction of your career – rent your house out and go on a training course? Move to somewhere totally new? Take a step back in seniority to get into a different kind of work? Take that promotion even though you are unsure that you can really do the job being offered?'

You should end up with more clarity on what you need to do *now* to try to make your future ambition a reality. And whether your horizon is five or ten years, you should be in no doubt about the likely impact of global population trends on our working lives. The 2016 book *The 100-Year Life* was based on the premise that the majority of children currently being born in rich countries could expect to survive beyond their hundredth birthday. And yet our societies and the policies of most governments remain rooted in the way previous generations have lived.[3] The gerontologist Professor Sarah Harper points out the profound change represented by the ageing of an entire population: 'To grow old in a society where most people are young is fundamentally different from doing so in a society where most people are old.'[4]

That's because of another shift taking hold at the same time. The decline in fertility rates that began in the richest countries of the world is spreading fast through Asia, Latin America and Africa. Women nearly everywhere are having fewer children and by 2100 those under fifteen are projected to make up less than 15 per cent of the global population. By 2050, when the UK is projected to have half a million citizens aged one hundred or more, Professor Harper says 'old age' will probably be a term associated with people in their late eighties or nineties and we will likely think less in terms of chronological age and more in terms of frailty or disability.[5]

The 100-Year Life co-author, Professor Lynda Gratton, agrees on the immense impact of these changes. 'We need to move away from this idea that life is three stages: full-time education, full-time work, full-time retirement,' she says. 'Instead, we should think of it much more as multi-stage, where we come in and out of work.'[6] That could well mean a greater convergence between the working lives of men and women: as professional life is stretched out by a decade or more, periods of maternity leave or working part-time should start to appear more marginal. The intense period that many women experience in their thirties, as they feel the pressure to establish themselves professionally and start families, may ease. We'll probably all think less in terms of 'a single career' and more about multiple careers or simply applying experience and skills to tasks and circumstances.

planning

We will also have to think differently about key moments to encourage aspiration and foster ambition, rethinking this as an ongoing, almost lifelong mission. Nevertheless, it will always be one that begins with the young and we know from the science on stereotyping as well as from surveys how horizons can be limited early on. In 2018 the Drawing the Future survey, involving 20,000 children aged seven to eleven from 20 countries, highlighted how gender, background and ethnicity can play a powerful role in children's ideas of their own potential. It found that jobs were often stereotyped by gender, career choices were made on the basis of these stereotypes and that children's aspirations are most influenced by who they know – their parents and their parents' friends – as well as by television and the media.[7]

From seeing the work of the charity Mosaic, I know how important it can be to provide first-hand accounts of the world of work that are wider than what children commonly see. Asking young professionals to volunteer their time, Mosaic sends them in to schools in disadvantaged communities where they mentor small groups over the course of an academic year. The task is to inspire the children about what their futures could be. 'They are growing up in communities where the very idea of work is quite often limited to something others do,' says Nizam Uddin, who leads Mosaic. 'Even where there are adults in close proximity to these young people who *are* in work, these are not the jobs that inspire them or the ones they marvel at from afar.' One British Asian mentor told me that the girls she worked with were amazed that someone from a background similar to theirs could grow up to be an independent woman, earning her own living.

The lawyer Miriam González Durántez founded an organisation called Inspiring Girls with a similar mission, taking female role models into schools. She thinks that the early teens are a key time to focus on girls. 'No matter whether they come from a city or a rural area, from a well-off background or not, self-confidence is an issue. Something happens when they are twelve to fifteen that knocks their confidence down. In my view it is the result of sexism that they begin to notice from the age of six.' A mother of three, she has also noticed how often she is asked about whether it is possible to combine a career and a family. 'This surprises me because I honestly don't think I was worried about that when I was thirteen. But they are already thinking about it and it is limiting them.'[8] According to a 2016 survey, as they get older, girls also increasingly perceive boys to have a better chance of success in their future jobs. While most seven- to ten-year-old girls thought their chances were equal to boys', that dropped to 54 per cent for eleven- to sixteen-year-olds and just 35 per cent among those aged seventeen to twenty-one.[9]

You also need to feel that an occupation that piques your interest would be open to you. 'You need to see it to be it' is a powerful maxim and I don't think I would ever have changed tack from law to journalism without seeing newspaper by-lines and television faces that resonated with me: Trevor McDonald, Zeinab Badawi, Yasmin Alibhai-Brown, George Alagiah, Gary Younge. Their presence was proof that people from an ethnic minority background could and did succeed in journalism, and without them I would not have had confidence that the media was open to someone with a name like mine.

Aiming for the media felt like a risk, however: less predictable than the law, or medicine, which my parents had hoped I would go into. Once I had decided that I would give journalism a go, I engaged in my first proper bit of career planning – not exactly a five-year plan but a concerted effort to build on the one bit of journalism I had done – interning for a newspaper in Pakistan during my gap year.

Knowing I needed to gather whatever work experience I could in print, radio or television, I sat in my university careers office, compiling lists of newspapers, magazines, broadcasters and production companies, and writing to them. I noted down names in the credits of television programmes I liked and wrote to the then BBC Legal Affairs Correspondent, Joshua Rozenberg, who very kindly let me shadow him for the day. Nowadays the BBC has a proper work experience scheme to give equal access to all applicants, but then it was all more piecemeal. In fact, everything I did in this period felt piecemeal, but gradually I gathered enough under my belt to have the beginnings of a journalism-focused CV.

I also discovered that this was indeed the field I wanted to be in, and after two years at Bloomberg News I joined the BBC in 1998. After that I experienced both intense phases when I found myself in demand and others when it felt as though I was stuck in a rut. But I tried to always have both an immediate horizon – doing my current job to the best of my ability – and a medium-term one, which was focused on what I wanted to be doing in five years' time. It meant I had an eye on the future, but not so much that I was distracted from my job by thinking about what else might be out there. Sometimes the time-frame I had in mind for a new opportunity came and went without anything materialising, and I had to adjust my hopes and expectations accordingly.

Today, I think of it as distilling ambition to fit where you are now, as well as provide a path to the next step. In my field, you might enter with the dream of one day becoming the editor of a major programme, but you'd still need to work backwards and figure out what you need to do to build up the best possible experience. Or you might join a big company and work your way up from a junior role, only to realise that a smaller operation with more scope for responsibility would suit you better. Having that second horizon can also be a way of seeing the difficult aspects of your job as a means to an end – if you know that this experience will reap a dividend in a few years' time it might just make the tricky boss, the long hours or the tiring commute a touch more bearable.

The careers and workplace expert Penny de Valk sees that twin-track approach as a way of 'thinking big while also being prepared for slow-burn development'. She once conducted a survey which suggested that fewer women than men engage in career planning, something she feels should not be the case. 'Luck favours the well prepared. Don't fret about "having it all" straight away, think about what's most important to you at this time in your life. Careers are a marathon these days, not a sprint.'[10]

The most challenging of my own phases of work came in the period after my second maternity leave, when I struggled to see how I might achieve the break I wanted into UK news programmes. I was far from unhappy at BBC World News, in fact I loved the international focus. But I had been there for several years and worried I was becoming too comfortable. There were no apparent openings on the programmes I regarded as the pinnacle of interviewing – *Today* and *Newsnight* – but I began to watch and listen to them in a different, more active way. As the interviewee spoke, I found myself imagining being on the other end of the conversation and thinking about how I would follow up. What would my next question be? How would I have handled a particular awkwardness or argument? It meant I was listening in a more engaged active manner than before.

The rugby coach Eddie Jones says something similar about how he behaves when watching sports or matches where he is not personally involved – the cricket for example. 'When you're a coach you put yourself in the situation – what would you be saying now to the batsman, what would you be saying if you were bowling now? It's the way you keep learning.'[11]

Longer working lives mean we will all need to maintain that learning and aspiration over a greater period of time. Five-year plans might help, but there will always be times when the reality turns out to be different, for better or worse. When I got my first job at Bloomberg TV, then just setting up in the UK, it was after applying and getting nowhere with a variety of entry-level posts and trainee schemes at British newspapers and broadcasters. My heart wasn't in the financial news in which Bloomberg had made its reputation, but my time there allowed me to develop skills which I realised later would never have been possible had I gone straight from university to somewhere more established. It was at Bloomberg that I had the chance to get my face and voice on air for the first time, recording some weekend bulletins from a newsroom camera booth with a self-operated autocue. The performance was entirely forgettable, but it stayed with me. When I had the chance to present at the BBC some years later, even that tiny bit of experience made me think: 'I've had a go at this before, I can do it again.'

In Brief

Develop a five-year plan

Think about what you want to be doing in a few years' time. It may seem an age away when you are just starting out, but the time goes quicker than you can imagine. Do you want to be one rung up the ladder in your current company? Or do you want to have moved sideways into another department, or to another employer, maybe somewhere bigger? Or perhaps you hope to be in an entirely different line of work by then? Having a plan shouldn't make you inflexible or close off opportunities but it can give you a sense of purpose and guard against drift.

Twin horizons

Be focused on where you want to go next but don't slip up on what you are doing now. You might be in a role that is not only far from your dream job but at a much lower level than you think you should be in – or just not what you want to be doing at all. Even so, try to pull out all the stops. Be the person who gives their utmost, whatever their role. It's that attitude that will help identify you as someone worthy of promotion, development or the trust of colleagues. So think in terms of twin horizons.

Learn from the experiences of others

In my world, this means listening to an interview and thinking actively about how I would respond to the contributor – what question would I follow up with? For those in sport, it means watching in the most active way possible when they are on the sidelines – picking up ideas from what they see others face on the court or pitch. Whatever your field, thinking through what you would do when faced with the dilemmas or trials of your peers or competitors will help you expand your understanding. The same scenario is unlikely to occur in your own life in exactly the same way, but seize the opportunity to develop your judgement through others' experience as well as your own.

Preparation

It is a narrow mind which cannot look at a subject from various points of view

George Eliot

A few months before he left office, President Obama delivered the graduation address at Rutgers University in New Jersey, telling students about to make their way out into the world that they would find it a much better place than it was when he finished university in the early 1980s. The fall of the Iron Curtain, the end of apartheid, reductions in poverty and disease were all evidence of that, and the world was more interconnected than ever before.

'Today in every phone in one of your pockets we have access to more information than at any time in human history, at a touch of a button,' he said. 'But, ironically, the flood of information hasn't made us more discerning of the truth. In some ways, it's just made us more confident in our ignorance. We assume whatever is on the web must be true. We search for sites that just reinforce our own predispositions.' Instead, he asked the students to put facts, reason and logic at the heart of how they saw the world: 'In politics and in life, ignorance is not a virtue.'[1]

Gauging the credibility of information is the cornerstone of my own professional life, but as we think about skills for a multi-stage life, it is also a vital starting point for the acquisition of all kinds of knowledge. A solid base of information, from which you can make robust assessments and good judgements, is an immense source of confidence. In two decades in journalism I've seen the significant change in how news is put together and transmitted on a variety of platforms. But the questions we ask about sources and material at different stages of the production process have remained more constant, the building blocks of a credible product and ever more important in contentious times.

When I joined the BBC as a junior producer, cutting even a ten-second sequence of pictures for a headline was a laborious process, beginning with finding the original tape of the footage and taking it to the rather forbidding domain of the video editors, who would cut the shots together and dub them onto a new tape. We would invariably then have to sprint down the corridor to get the pictures to the output side of the operation in time for them to be played out on air. Now, producers can view and edit footage from their desktops, but they're likely to be bombarded with a multitude of possible material, including 'citizen journalism', YouTube videos and social media comments and trends.

As consumers, the information load – or overload – can give us the illusion of being much more knowledgeable than we really are. We may not even be aware of how our internet experience can be so personalised that it reduces what we see. Eli Pariser, author of the book *Filter Bubble*, gives the example of asking two friends to Google the word 'Egypt' and send him screenshots of the results. One image was dominated by news stories and headlines such as 'Crisis in Egypt', because of protests that were underway at that time. The other showed little evidence of that, dominated instead by information about tourism and the historic sites of the country.

Why did the two men – who both did the search from the United States – get such different results? All tech companies are careful in what they reveal about the programming behind their services, but Google often says its goal is to provide useful and *relevant* search results.[2] Pariser used the Egypt example to show that what we may think of as a purely objective search, using key words to tap into a mammoth database of knowledge, also involves choices being made for us. 'Your filter bubble is your own personal, unique universe of information that you live in online. And what's in your filter bubble depends on who you are, and it depends on what you do. But the thing is that you don't decide what gets in. And more importantly, you don't actually see what gets edited out.' As far as the news media is concerned, he says the idea that the internet

Scott's search

Daniel's search

sweeping away gatekeepers of information – editors – is a positive phenomenon is misplaced: 'What we're seeing is more of a passing of the torch from human gatekeepers to algorithmic ones. And the algorithms don't yet have the kind of embedded ethics that the editors did.'[3]

For many millions of people who use Facebook, the algorithms of its News Feed have a profound influence on what they see of the world. This is the core stream of information visible to the user, which the company says is 'meant to keep you connected to the people, places and things that you care about'.[4] It has been central to its commercial success because data on how long we spend on Facebook helps make the case to advertisers that it is worth their product or service being on there too. In 2018, after criticism that Facebook had exposed millions of Americans to divisive messages and 'fake news' stories emanating from Russia, the algorithm was tweaked to focus on content posted by users' family and friends rather than media, brands or other third parties.[5] But, of course, there is a high degree of probability that our family and our friends have a similar worldview to our own – what they share is likely to chime rather than contrast with our own beliefs.

More pernicious is where algorithms act as censors, stifling the sharing of news. In the summer of 2014, when demonstrations began in Ferguson, Missouri, in the wake of the police killing of the unarmed black teenager Michael Brown, the sociologist Zeynep Tufekci noticed a striking difference in what she was seeing on her Facebook and Twitter feeds. It was then the fourth night after Brown's death, and while she could see her Twitter stream alive with details of the anger in Ferguson, her Facebook feed – where she was friends with a similar set of people – was silent on the subject. The next morning she noticed that her Facebook friends *had* been writing and sharing material about Ferguson at the time, but for some reason the posts did not appear in her feed for another twelve hours.

Tufekci, who is an assistant professor at the University of North Carolina, thought they might have become prominent only as more people engaged with them, which raises important questions about how stories emerge into the public consciousness. Michael Brown's death and the way the protests were policed ended up sparking outrage and demonstrations across the US, but Tufekci's analysis showed that it could have been otherwise. 'Algorithmic filtering, as a layer, controls what you see on the Internet,' she wrote. 'What if Ferguson had started to bubble, but there was no Twitter to catch on nationally? What happens to #Ferguson affects what happens to Ferguson.'[6]

Twitter, too, can be an echo chamber, unless you make a point of choosing to follow a wide range of people. It can be enraging to see views with which you vehemently disagree pop up on your timeline. But being exposed to a broad spectrum of opinion leaves you better placed to make your own judgements, and support them with evidence. 'Use your logic and reason and words,' said Barack Obama at Rutgers. 'By doing so, you'll strengthen your own position, and you'll hone your arguments. And maybe you'll learn something and realize you don't know everything. And you may have a new understanding not only about what your opponents believe but maybe what you believe.'

In my daily working life, colleagues, contributors or audience reaction might all play a role in what makes me pause and re-evaluate an assertion, a phrase or even the use of a single word. One morning on the radio, I referred to the migrant camp then in existence outside Calais as 'the jungle'. It was a commonly used term at the time, but I then saw that the journalist Joseph Harker had tweeted me, attaching a piece he had written on the subject. In it, he argued that even though the name had first been used by the occupants themselves, as a way of describing their grim living conditions, its continuing use dehumanised them. It meant that questions about them hung in the air: 'What kind of people live in a jungle? Are they civilised? Are they respectable?'[7]

The era of 'fake news' has brought a new urgency to the

need to think critically and make an objective analysis of whatever is before you. It might be something that is demonstrably false – one sensational-looking story about Hillary Clinton in 2016, headlined 'FBI Agent Suspected in Hillary Email Leaks Found Dead in Apparent Murder-Suicide', purported to come from the *Denver Guardian*, a publication that a few clicks would have established did not actually exist.[8] 'In the past, when you needed information, you went to an encyclopedia and you could trust that the information would be true,' says Andreas Schleicher, who runs the PISA system of tests for fifteen-year-olds in dozens of countries and believes schools should be teaching children to spot fake news.[9]

That is one starting point. What is more complex is developing a mindset that appreciates the value of other points of view and the right to hold them, while still being prepared to listen, engage and keep an open mind. When the terrorism and security expert Professor Louise Richardson became the first woman vice-chancellor of Oxford University in 2016, she spoke of the challenge of educating students so they are prepared for jobs that cannot even be imagined today: 'If we continue to do what we do best we will inevitably help the country manage its future. If we can provide leaders for tomorrow who have been educated to think critically, to act ethically and always to question, these are the people who will prevent the next financial crisis; who will help us to grapple with the fundamental questions prompted by the accelerating pace of technological change.'[10]

All of this begins with casting the information net as wide as possible and building a base of information that will be robust enough to help make judgements about veracity and reliability, impartiality and opinion. It might begin with just five minutes of news while you're getting dressed in the morning, a cursory scroll through headlines on a reputable app, or adding news providers to your social media feeds. Or, spotting patterns of coverage and areas of interest for newspapers or news websites – what stories are featuring and how does the emphasis vary? Why might that be – who runs, funds or owns that particular publication? If you're curating this right, you should see stories that make you nod in agreement and others that spike your blood pressure or challenge what you think you know.

You can mine different platforms for a variety of content: Facebook is where I often find great video that I would not otherwise have seen, particularly inspirational real-life stories; Instagram regularly alerts me to new books, trends and products; Twitter is a fantastic shortcut to wider reading, as people recommend and share links to articles; Wikipedia an invaluable starting point when I need to look something up.

But where you're planning to rely on the information

you find – check and cross-check. Wikipedia is quite open about the fact that the nature of its model – information inputted by thousands of volunteer editors – means that the quality of content is variable, saying 'We do not expect you to trust us.'[11] And I have a personal reminder of that: the birthday listed for me on my own Wikipedia page makes me a month older than I actually am. I once asked Jimmy Wales, the site's founder, whether I should try and correct it – not really, he said, because editing your own Wikipedia page is frowned upon. And so there the error remains, at least at the time of writing.

Some misleading material is deliberately put into the public domain, but there are also errors that could have easily been avoided. In August 2017, Turkey's deputy prime minister Mehmet Şimsek tweeted about the Rohingya refugee crisis, saying it amounted to ethnic cleansing, and including four pictures of suffering people. He then had to apologise and delete the tweet when it became apparent that none of the four pictures could be proven to be from the events then unfolding on the Myanmar border – one turned out to have been taken in Rwanda in 1994, another in Indonesia in 2003. And yet at the time there was no shortage of verifiable images of the Rohingyas' desperate plight.[12] In another incident, Kenneth Roth, the director of the campaign group Human Rights Watch, tweeted about President Trump's choice for deputy director of the CIA being a 'woman who ran a CIA black site for torture'. The accompanying picture was not, however, one of Gina Haspel but BBC presenter Emily Maitlis.

Sometimes, a quick look back at the original source material provides a different picture of a particular assertion. In the summer of 2016, when Jeremy Corbyn was in the middle of his campaign for re-election as leader of the Labour Party, a website called Corbyn Facts countered criticism that he had failed to put enough time or effort into delivering a 'Remain' vote in the EU referendum that had just taken place. In fact, it said, he had given 122 speeches during the campaign. When Radio 4's statistics programme *More or Less* looked into the claim, it discovered it was based on a Loughborough University analysis that had counted appearances in the media rather than speeches delivered in the six-week run-up to the vote. 'Appearances' were defined as anything from substantial coverage to a mere reference to a particular person in a newspaper or a glimpse of them on one of the main television news programmes. *More or Less* presenter Tim Harford concluded that the '122 speeches' cited on the Corbyn Facts website were in truth 122 *mentions* of Jeremy Corbyn – and that these could be mentions of any kind, even saying that he hadn't been seen much on the campaign trail.[13]

When it comes to news, every journalist wants their

work to stand out, but the wider context is not always present. Take reports on the surge in vinyl music sales for instance – in one week in 2016 they were said to have exceeded the value of digital downloads. A vintage format making a remarkable comeback? Partly true, but the large sales in that specific week were mostly due to its popularity as a Christmas present.[14] The big picture for the music industry is that physical sales are declining and that streaming services have overtaken downloads of individual singles and albums – a change with serious implications for record labels and artists.[15]

Reporting health-related research can require particular responsibility. In 2016, the *Sun* newspaper ran a front-page story headlined 'Vaping as Bad as Fags'. But the study it was based on involved just twenty-four patients,[16] while the way it was written up omitted the broader context of known harm, or that public health advice on e-cigarettes is framed around their use as a means of quitting smoking.[17]

Check, double-check, question. I couldn't conduct a decent interview without a solid grasp of the facts, but I also need another, much more underrated ability – to listen properly to the answers. It sounds obvious, but all too often, an interviewee says something that is not picked up – sometimes because there was no more time, or it would take the conversation in an unwanted direction, but also on occasion because the interviewer simply didn't hear it.

I regularly remind myself to listen intently, and also think back to advice from one of my editors early in my presenting career. It was given in the context of a breaking news situation, when there might be a flood of incoming information and you need to grasp whatever facts are available, keeping hold of them as the story develops. 'Write down what the reporter tells you,' she said. And I do. Even a few words can really help maintain focus in a newsroom scrambling to get the latest information on air. In other settings, it won't always feel appropriate to be scribbling something down at the time, but doing so immediately afterwards means you have a near-contemporaneous record.

Making sure you pause to absorb also slows down the process of reacting to what you have heard. That is valuable even in the most senior roles – perhaps more so. The American businessman Doug Conant, who turned around the fortunes of the Campbell Soup Company, advocates a 'listen-frame-advance' approach to remind executives not to move ahead too quickly. 'Leaders have a bias for action,' he says. 'When they're listening, it may not feel like they're accomplishing anything. Nothing could be further from the truth. Listening intently helps you figure out what is really going on and what others need from you. It's a way to demonstrate that you genuinely care. Framing the issue ensures that everyone has the same understanding. Advancing the agenda means deciding what next steps to take and who will take them.'[18]

Even if you're not the one deciding what those next steps will be, there is something to take away from this. If you can ground what you say in the words you have just heard, reinforcing the point made to you or rooting your own in the same terms, it is evidence that you have paid proper attention. You might do this in a question, perhaps by prefacing it with 'When you say …' and going on to ask what you want to know. And regardless of the content, the mere act of asking can fill the time and build the perception of an interested, engaged, curious person. And that might just be what sets you apart.

In Brief

Cast your information net wide

We have access to so much information at the touch of a button, but we can easily exist in bubbles where our understanding of the world is rarely challenged. Success in the workplace means being able to anticipate what's coming down the road: the problem that's bubbling, the trend with far-reaching implications, the threat to a business. Without being exposed to how other people think and what they believe, our capacity for agile judgements and decision-making is reduced. One easy way to fix this is through social media – following people who surprise and enrage you as well as those you agree with.

Check and cross-check

Get into the habit of verifying anything you are going to rely on, and being ready to back up your assertions with evidence. Some information is put into the public domain with the intent of misleading or influencing in a malign way, but failing to check things out properly can also mean errors that will reflect badly on you personally or professionally.

Listen with intent

One of the most under-appreciated abilities is that of proper listening – rather than letting what you are hearing wash over you. Sometimes the task is difficult because people are hinting or speaking in code, and their true meaning is unclear, but far more often we hear what we want to, or we do not focus properly. I try to listen as actively as I can, almost imprinting the key words onto my brain.

Starting Out

No matter what your current ability is,
effort is what ignites that ability and
turns it into accomplishment

Carol Dweck

How do you demonstrate a keen intent and a sense of purpose, not only for an instant but more broadly, particularly in your first years in the workplace or in a new job? This is when expectations and judgements can be made frighteningly quickly, and the impression left by inexperience or an early mistake can be hard to shake off.

One well-known psychological experiment of the 1960s suggested that in the first years of primary school the expectations of teachers could have a significant effect on the academic attainment of children. In what they called 'Pygmalion in the Classroom', researchers Robert Rosenthal and Lenore Jackson told teachers at a California school at the start of an academic year that some of the children in their classes had been identified through IQ tests as 'spurters' – likely to outperform the others. The teachers were given the names of children in this group and, sure enough, at the end of the year they were found to have done better than their peers.

In truth, the names given to the teachers of the 'spurter' children had been chosen at random. So why did this group of children in the experiment outperform the others in the class? The authors of the study believed their results showed how 'one person's expectations of another's behavior may come to serve as a self-fulfilling prophecy. When teachers expected that certain children would show greater intellectual development, those children did show greater intellectual development.'[1] It was a striking conclusion, albeit one later questioned by others, who pointed out that the control group also showed gains in IQ and that the differences between the two sets of results were small.[2]

Much more recently the work of psychologist Carol Dweck, with its emphasis on the development of intelligence rather than on exceptionalism, has been influential on education and elsewhere. 'Our society worships talent, and many people assume that possessing superior intelligence or ability – along with confidence in that ability – is a recipe for success,' she says. 'In fact, however, more than thirty-five years of scientific investigation suggests that an overemphasis on intellect or talent leaves people vulnerable to failure, fearful of challenges and unwilling to remedy their shortcomings.'[3]

In her own studies, she tried to work out why some children persevered in the face of tough assignments while others gave up. In one, she and her research associate Carol Diener asked ten- and eleven-year-olds to think aloud while they tried to solve a set of problems. Some associated the difficulties they experienced with their own limitations – for example, that they didn't have a good memory – while others seemed to relish the going getting tough. This second group outperformed the others.[4]

Over time she developed her ideas and observations into a theory that the first set of learners perceived their intelligence and talent as set in place, which she called a 'fixed mindset', while the second had a 'growth mindset', believing their abilities could be developed over time. 'They're not always worried about how smart they are, how they'll look, what a mistake will mean. They challenge themselves and grow.'[5]

In another experiment, a group of twelve- and thirteen-year-olds were taught that intelligence was malleable, that learning forms new connections in the brain and that students themselves are in charge of this process. When the marks achieved by this group of children in maths were then tracked, they were found to have improved. Those of children in a control group, who had not been taught the theory, declined.[6]

It was through maths that I first came across Professor Dweck's work, when my children started using the remarkable and free online maths resource Khan Academy. Its founder Sal Khan believes passionately in the mindset approach to learning and put it into practice with his own child. 'I decided to praise my son not when he succeeded at things he was already good at, but when he persevered with things that he found difficult,' he says. 'I stressed to him that by struggling, your brain grows.' Khan knew he had got through when one night his five-year-old, reading aloud, stumbled over a new word: '"Dad, aren't you glad how I struggled with that word?" he asked. "I think I could feel my brain growing."'[7] On his website, Sal Khan also found that messages praising users' tenacity resulted in them spending more time learning on it.

At any stage in life, we develop the scope of our ability by tackling the harder problems or tasks before us. In my world that means the interview with the Cabinet minister rather than the straightforward on-air conversation with a correspondent – the former will be more daunting, harder to predict and a far greater test than the latter. For others it might mean the presentation they're dreading, the meeting they would ideally like to put off, volunteering to take on the tougher client or opting to work with the more exacting boss.

These harder options are all likely to teach you more than their easier alternatives, in a way that would be impossible to emulate in the abstract. Being willing to do this from your first interactions with colleagues will demonstrate intent in the crucial period in which you establish yourself in their eyes – as well as develop your own sense of professional self-worth.

In a new role or company, you'd want to demonstrate from the very first day that you have arrived with as good an understanding as is possible from the outside – the customers of the company, the audience you're trying to reach, the issues facing that particular industry, the stresses your bosses might be under. Maybe their business model hasn't delivered, they are threatened by competitors or being disrupted by new services, technologies or products. What might you mention that shows you are in tune with what they're dealing with? Early on, try to be noticed for a particular observation or insight, a piece of work, an idea. Employers and peers can make very swift decisions about the value you represent and what you bring to the role, but your aim should be to establish positive credentials, even for just one thing. If and when something goes wrong later on, you will hopefully have some credit to draw upon and to cushion you.

Some new beginnings or projects require more of a deep dive. When I was asked to be one of the presenters of the

BBC's Olympics coverage in 2012, I had assumed that I would be paired up with a sports broadcaster and be part of a double act – my expertise being on the news side and theirs on the events and the competition. When the schedule was revealed shortly before the Games it turned out to be rather different – I was to have a solo morning slot on national television throughout the Olympics, fronting three hours of wall-to-wall sport. I was taken aback: how could I hold my own alongside specialist broadcasters of the calibre of Sue Barker, Hazel Irvine, Clare Balding, Gary Lineker or Gabby Logan?

It was instantly clear that I would have to do some serious homework. The Games would involve three weeks on air, having to be ready to talk about any Olympic sport with an understanding of its rules and history, the runners and riders and where different countries' hopes would rest. All of this in front of the large audiences expected for a unique national event.

There was considerable potential for me to be horribly exposed, but equally I couldn't pretend be what I wasn't or morph into a sports journalist. I began the only way that made sense to me, buying a book on the Olympics and a large notebook and reading up on each event. There were obvious judgements to make along the way – more focus on those where Britain's chances were good and those where the competition would be taking place during the times when I would be on air, but also information about venues and medal contenders. My notebook started to fill up, and once the Games were underway, it came with me every morning to the studio. In the end, I rarely needed to open it, but I knew it was there and it gave me confidence. A few days into the competition, I looked down one morning from the piled-up shipping containers that served as the BBC studios onto the spectators filling the park below and realised I was relishing every moment.

I tried to do a mini-version of the same the following year, ahead of starting on *Today*. This would be a considerable shift in several ways – getting used to radio but also the agenda, because I had spent most of my career focused on international news rather than the UK. I wanted to make as good a start as possible, knowing that negative feedback early on would add an extra layer of stress to what was sure to be an unnerving experience.

I spent as much time as I could shadowing the programme, seeing how the presenters and the team worked, trying to soak up as much of the mechanics of the operation as possible, so that when the time came I could better focus on the content. And then I closeted myself away for a few days with a long reading list. It was never going to be a complete brief on what I needed to know, but it was my own way of getting into the right mindset for a new beginning.

For most people, the route towards any new beginning will start with the form-filling stage of a recruitment process or a CV. Some of those I have looked at over the years have immediately portrayed the individuals concerned in a good light. Others made my heart sink – spelling mistakes, loose phrasing, messy layouts giving the impression that not enough care has been taken, sometimes a silly, inappropriate email address based on the candidate's nickname. Once a BBC team I was with on location had taken someone on to help out with logistics and setting up interviews. A few days in we realised that the email address he was using on the team's behalf was a combination of his first name and 'pistol'. All he had needed to do was set up a sensible one for work purposes, but it had probably never crossed his mind.

When you're starting out, a one-page CV is all you need and – depending on what you are applying for – you might have more than one version of it. Be judicious about what goes into each one, so that as much of the content as possible is relevant to the position being aimed for and backs up rather than distracts from the impression you are trying to create. That may mean leaving out some experiences, a process that will become more important as time goes on. You might well have more that could go on the CV, but it doesn't mean that everything should.

Often, getting someone else to look over it will result in some quick fixes: ways in which a mission or personal statement at the top could be tightened up or better phrased, spotting typos or grammatical errors. Amending font, spacing and layout can all help enhance the look of the content, helping the experience detailed to stand out.

More active words can have the same effect – 'developed', 'designed', 'implemented' rather than 'worked on' or 'completed'. All of this will apply even where first-stage recruitment is done on the basis of a standardised form, as some employers prefer. You may have more space available and be able to version parts of the CV – the statement perhaps – into something more expansive. But even if you're writing in paragraphs rather than bullet points, try to make every word earn its place in the text. Your experience should jump out and be easy for the reader to absorb.

Make sure you're familiar with precisely how each stage of recruitment works for the positions you're going for, because there may be considerable variation. At the law firm Clifford Chance, biographical details of candidates are removed before the final stage of applications to become one of its UK trainees. Laura King, the partner responsible for recruitment, says the change was made after concern about bias formation: 'When we queried interviewers as to what they did with the CV information they received, we found they generally read it relatively quickly pre-meeting and were looking for things they might have in common with the candidate, such as a school or sport.' Providing only a name also had the knock-on benefit of not overloading the interviewers with paperwork, which saved a considerable amount of time given that the firm typically runs large interview days involving hundreds of applicants.

At the *Spectator* magazine, candidates for internships write a covering letter detailing any relevant experience and complete tasks aimed at revealing their aptitude for journalism – story ideas, sample blog posts or analysis of a news event. It's a process that should make the playing field more level, and while applications come mostly from younger people seeking an entry into the media, there can be some unexpected results.

In 2017, one of those gaining an internship was a forty-eight-year-old mother of three, Katherine Forster, seeking a new direction after fifteen years of looking after her children: 'Our culture assumes that no one over forty starts at the bottom. But why not? Why should it be funny when we try?' she later wrote. 'Surely the funny thing is that more people don't do it, and that many companies only recruit from one age group.' She wondered why employers don't give more thought to people like her, an untapped mass of potential workers. 'There are millions of women in Britain who have had a great education, who have focused on their families but who now have more time and a lot to give professionally.'[8]

Some employers do offer 'returnships' or similar schemes aimed at opening a path back to the workplace after people have taken time out. But even after just a few months on maternity leave, returning can be daunting and stressful, as I know from my own experience. There are layers of worries: do you have the right childcare in place? Who's been filling in for you? Might they have done a better job? This is also the point at which you might be making decisions with far-reaching implications for pay and progression, such as going part-time. It's far from easy to have to establish yourself in your colleagues' eyes all over again, at a time when you may have little flexibility on staying an extra hour or going the extra mile because of the other demands on your life. The work trip that might previously have been a perk and a welcome change from normal routine suddenly feels like a logistical nightmare, and possibly an expensive one if it involves paying for extra childcare.

Add to that the personal worries you may have about the needs of those closest to you. In 2005, I was standing in a supermarket aisle buying cake decorations for my son's first birthday when I was asked to go to Pakistan to cover the terrible earthquake that had just taken place. One voice in my head told me I should go, that he was too little to know what a birthday was. It was countered by another: 'What will I say when he asks why his mother isn't in his first birthday pictures?' After my twins were born, work travel of any kind was hard to contemplate, which was far from ideal for someone in international news. I did start travelling again within a few years, but was grateful not to have been written off by my editors in the meantime.

One executive in the male-dominated field of oil and gas told me how he realised that job advertisements including the phrase 'frequent travel required' were a significant stumbling block to his efforts to recruit women into his department. Ayman Assaf was running IT services at BP in 2015 when he decided he had to get beyond the fait accompli usually put to him, that women simply didn't go for technical roles. He was particularly keen to get women into technical architecture – the design and development of IT systems and networks – as well as into his leadership team.

When he looked at the text of advertisements sent out for those positions, he saw at once how the same wording was used again and again. 'Whenever there was a vacancy, the same job description was taken out and dusted off a little bit. A few details were changed and it was posted.' One of the perennial requirements stated that travel would be required for 25 per cent of the employee's time. When

Assaf thought about it, he realised that in truth, very few people in the company would spend a whole week a month travelling. It was a standard term that did not reflect the reality of most employees' experience. But it would be likely to put off women – and men – who had childcare responsibilities or simply didn't relish the idea of spending that much time away from home.

In came the replacement phrase 'Travel if necessary'. And when Assaf thought about how the technical architects worked, he realised something else: the roles could operate as a pool, with individuals choosing to do different numbers of days. They were also well suited to agile working – flexibility on when and where the work was carried out. That term went into the new advertisements too, and the number of women applicants went up. When it came to the interview, he made sure to bring up the flexible-working possibilities: 'Sometimes people don't believe what they see in the job description. So at the interview I would say: "By the way, it's agile and we mean it." I remember the relief in one candidate's face when she said "I live in Wimbledon. Can I work from Wimbledon?" And I said yes.'

Digging deeper into the wording of recruitment, he and his team looked at other elements that might alienate good candidates. They replaced words that might be perceived as particularly masculine with ones that were more neutral:

'able' in the place of 'strong', and 'committed' in the place of 'determined'. The behavioural economist Iris Bohnet, who has written a book about designing systems for equality rather than trying to train people out of their biases, says the approach applies equally to words most often used for women. 'When I want to increase the fraction of male teachers, I should not use adjectives that in our minds are typically associated with women, such as compassionate, warm, supportive, caring,' she says. It is not that men cannot have those qualities, but their strong association with women decreases the chances of men applying. A primary school wanting to recruit men would therefore be better served, she says, by a job description seeking simply 'an excellent teacher with exceptional pedagogical skills' rather than 'A committed teacher with exceptional pedagogical and interpersonal skills to work in a supportive, collaborative work environment.'[9]

In the university sector, Professor Athene Donald says there is considerable debate about gendered language in recruitment: 'We often advertise using terms such as "world-leading" and "excellence", which probably deters women. Some are not going to put their hand up and say "I'm world-leading", even if they are. It's also completely unnecessary because the university can decide itself which applicant is "world-leading". It doesn't have to be specified in the advert.' Donald once complained to civil servants about the way in which they had advertised positions on a board advising the government on research and innovation, including the requirement to 'speak authoritatively', actively 'drive' work and pursue their mission. 'This isn't vocabulary everyone is likely to use,' she says. 'Indeed, many people, men and women, may not be comfortable thinking of themselves with those robust phrases. I know of some very senior women from the top echelons of Russell Group universities who told me they looked at the advertisement and decided it wasn't for them because of the language in which it was couched.'[10]

Iris Bohnet says the way to make processes fairer is to recognise the biases that we all have. She gives an example from her own life, when she took her baby son to a daycare centre. 'One of the first teachers I saw was a man. I wanted to turn and run. This *man* didn't conform to my expectations of what a preschool teacher looked like. Of course, he turned out to be a wonderful caregiver who later became a trusted babysitter at our house, but I couldn't help my initial gut reaction. I was sexist for only a few seconds, but it bothers me to this day.'[11]

In recruitment, she advocates using software that strips age, gender and educational background out of applications and then bringing structure and standardisation to the interview stage by using a prepared list of questions.

'The interviews pose the same set of questions in the same order to all candidates, allowing clearer comparisons between them. Of course, the flow of conversation during the interview will be slightly more awkward, but the payoff is worth it.'

The interviewer should score the candidate on each answer as it is given, rather than waiting until the meeting has come to an end. 'This neutralizes a variety of biases,' says Professor Bohnet. 'We are more likely to remember answers with vivid examples, and answers that are most recent. Evaluators who wait until the end of the interview to rate answers risk forgetting an early or less-vivid but high-quality answer, or favoring candidates whose speaking style favors storytelling.' She also advocates abandoning interview panels, believing that it's preferable for candidates to have a series of interviews with a single questioner each time, than one interview conducted by a group.

Some of this challenges my own long-held assumptions about what constitutes a good and fair process – candidates will be nervous, so you would think it is best to set them at their ease with a conversation that is as natural as possible rather than the rigidity of a list of questions. You might also assume that the diversity of thought represented by a panel of evaluators is preferable to a single judgement each time. But we need to go where the evidence takes us if we're serious about finding ways of operating that don't perpetuate the same imbalances into another generation.

In Brief

Getting in the right frame of mind for a new project

Try to set aside some time to immerse yourself in content that you know you need to be across ahead of a new role or endeavour. I did this in the runup to the 2012 Olympics, clearing the diary for a few days and taking a deep dive into unfamiliar material made a real difference, both to my knowledge and to my confidence.

The art of the CV or application form

Often these are written with a focus on job titles rather than what work you have actually done. Look at your experience afresh from the point of view of the person hiring in each job you are going for. Which bit of your experience is most relevant? Does it jump out enough? Can you use words to vividly describe what you did and what you would bring to that next role – 'developed', 'oversaw', 'established', 'implemented'? If you've been away from the workplace because of caring responsibilities or other reasons, don't gloss over it, make it clear that you are raring to go and ready to embark on a new phase of life.

Take job advertisements with a pinch of salt

These can be put together without much thought and tend to be full of stock phrases. If a job description looks right to you apart from a few details – for example, how much you need to travel for work – apply anyway. That part may well be negotiable and if you get the job, you can discuss it. Don't rule yourself out of potential opportunities too easily, if it's an internal role it can be important to be seen to go for it in order to show intent and potential. It may not work out but you'll be at the forefront of their minds next time.

Avoid big decisions at times of transition or change

Try to keep things as simple as possible at junctions such as returning from maternity leave. They are not easy and the practicalities and organisation of different aspects of life can be overwhelming. This is not the time to decide what you can or can't do at work in the long run. Take one day at a time.

Speaking Up

The human voice is the most perfect instrument of all

Arvo Pärt

What happens when a woman starts to speak? It's something I often have cause to think about because communication is at the heart of what I do. In the view of Christine Lagarde, a veteran of many high-profile gatherings over the years, women can get a less than attentive hearing. 'It's very often the case, particularly in male-dominated environments, that when a woman who is part of the group takes the floor, the attention of the men in the room goes down a few notches,' she told an audience in 2017, challenging them to observe it for themselves. 'They start doing something else – looking at their emails, or chatting with the person sitting next to them. It happens all the time.'

What should women do, she was asked, if they find themselves in that position? 'You can sink into your text, keep going and hope that it finishes as quickly as possible,' she said. 'I would not recommend that. Or, you can raise your voice so that people can actually hear you. One of the things I have found most effective is to pause, because people suddenly think that maybe something is wrong, and they pay attention again.'[1]

It is good advice, but her observation about seeing attention drift feeds into the nagging doubts that many of us have about public speaking: how will we perform when many sets of eyes are focused upon us? The doubts can be there whatever your field: contrary to what might be imagined of broadcasters, I found the experience of being before a physical audience extremely nerve-racking when I first began to receive speaking invitations. Unlike what I was accustomed to in a studio or on location, the 'viewers' were right there in front of me. It was a considerable adjustment to see the faces of those listening and, often, to be able to gauge from their expressions the reactions to what I was saying.

It is, however, an adjustment that must be made, given that it's hard to envisage a career path unlikely to involve addressing a group or larger audience at some stage, particularly as you rise in seniority. Preparing for these moments of scrutiny depends both on thinking through your content and the amount of practice you are willing to put in. But the vehicle for it all is the voice and it is one of which people often seem unsure – think of the frequency with which you hear the words 'I hate the way my voice sounds.' I felt that myself, even long after I started appearing on air, bothered in particular by the sound of my isolated voice; for example, in a voiceover for a television report.

Speaking to a camera, there are many ways to add life and emphasis to your words, even with the slightest, barely discernible furrowing of the brow or narrowing of the eyes. Working with the voice alone, none of these tools are available. And yet I swiftly learned how revealing the voice can be, from the tone used in introducing or questioning a contributor to where there are hesitations or interruptions. I have even learned to be mindful of the sound of my breathing, after once being told that a somewhat heavy breath I had taken sounded as though I was sighing at what the interviewee had said. Quite apart from that are the many speech-related pitfalls arising from a live programme with little opportunity to review and rephrase your thoughts until they are the best expression of what you want to convey.

For all of these reasons a speech that can be planned, structured and rehearsed in advance feels less perilous to me. But that is only because I have live broadcasting to compare it to. For all but the experienced public speaker it will still be a big moment, and like so many other endeavours, it will get easier – and better – the more times you do it. Yet for women, gaining that experience can be tricky, with keynote speaker slots as well as places on panel discussions often disproportionately filled by men.

From history, too, we are much more familiar with the image of a man addressing a group of people than a woman and the label of 'orator', lifting someone above being a mere speaker, is usually associated with men. The classicist Professor Mary Beard points out that rhetoric – language designed to persuade – was born from a world that excluded women: 'There is nowhere in the Ancient Mediterranean world where women had any political rights, there is no place that they could vote, they were always outside the system of persuasion that held the men together. One of the things that Western culture hasn't worked out is "What does a persuasive or an authoritative female voice actually sound like?"'[2]

On the air waves, although women are now well represented, they are still unlikely to be the main presenters of the most authoritative radio and television news programmes. It wasn't until 2006 that one of the three major US networks appointed a woman – Katie Couric – as the main anchor of an evening news programme. At the BBC, pioneering women had to battle to get beyond programming focused on 'household matters' and instructing their audience, especially children, in some way. In 1943, the then presentation director of the BBC, John Snagge, was asked why women didn't read the news.

It had been tried, he replied, but he didn't intend to repeat the experiment because 'a great many people' would not like it. 'We don't believe now is the time to re-open that controversy.'[3]

Opportunities increased during the Second World War, as they did in many industries when posts were vacant due to men being away fighting, but it was more of an interlude than the blossoming of a new era. In 1973, an internal BBC report aimed at unearthing what women at the organisation were up against found a range of views that the historian Jean Seaton says revealed the deep prejudice of the time: 'Women were not aggressive enough, didn't like competition, needed encouragement, had to look after other people, found the scrutiny if they did make it to a top job difficult, and did not get promoted because they did not do well enough earlier on.' Those on air were regarded as a risk to the BBC's impartiality, because it was thought they might break down while reading a particularly sad story.[4]

Elsewhere in society, the sound of a woman's voice could be perceived as a potential impediment to her progress. When Elizabeth Butler-Sloss, later Britain's first woman appeals court judge, began to think about a career in the law, her father told her she would have to calm down, slow down, and that her voice was too high. She took note – he was himself a judge and therefore knew the field he was talking about – and over time she worked on her speech, practising in front of the mirror.[5]

Margaret Thatcher, too, worked on her voice as part of a plan to change the way she came across, having been made all too aware that some regarded her as shrill. 'When she became Leader of the Opposition in 1975,' explains her biographer Charles Moore, 'Labour MPs used to make squeaking noises as she entered the House of Commons chamber, in imitation of her. She needed voice dominance to beat them.' A voice coach from the National Theatre was drafted in, and Thatcher dedicated considerable time and effort to the mission. 'She was extremely conscientious and rehearsed endlessly,' says Moore. 'Anything that would get the message across better was considered and usually accepted.'

Focusing on the pitch of women's voices is pretty outdated today, although the voice coach Elspeth Morrison says it hasn't disappeared altogether. 'The young women who come to me sometimes say they've been told their voice is too high,' she says. 'I ask them how old they are. And if they're twenty-two, chances are that their voice is absolutely appropriate for their age.' If they say they don't like the sound of their voice, she often finds that means they are self-conscious about their accent. 'My job is to assure them that the way they sound is fine,' she says. 'The only thing they may need is a little help with clarity, maybe with the odd vowel sound, in case people are unfamiliar with that particular accent.'

I got to know Elspeth in the run-up to the Olympics, when she helped me think about how voices have a natural variation, depending on the situation. 'Your voice with your children will be different to the one you use when calling a company to complain about a service, and different again to the voice you use in an interview. We alter how we communicate in order to get what we want.' Far from being self-conscious, she says women should take pride in the ease with which most of us do this without a second thought. 'We are conversation drivers and listeners and often the people who push conversations forward. So, we will chameleon in to whatever the situation requires. Our voices do go higher than men's voices around children, not because we are patronising them, but because children hear at higher frequencies.'

Rather than become self-conscious about the way we sound, Elspeth advocates thinking instead about diction and emphasis. All too often she hears people place the stress on the wrong words in a sentence when they're making a speech or broadcasting. 'Emphasis is not usually on nouns,' she says, giving an example to explain her point. 'People think that is the *way* with *words*. But in normal conversation, the emphasis tends to be on adjectives and the words we use to help describe an action or situation:

could, *should*, *maybe*. You need to think about the overall shape of what you want to say rather than focusing on your voice.'

When you look at a text ahead of delivering it, the words to emphasise might be obvious – but you can also amend so it is even clearer, by underlining words or putting them in bold or in italics. I do this for speeches and sometimes for my on-air scripts as well, customising with dashes, double dashes, an ellipsis – whatever I feel nudges me towards the tone I want to strike. Something you have written yourself is always more likely to be a natural fit with your speech pattern and sound better when read aloud, and if you can't practise aloud then it's worth going through it line by line and mouthing the words. You might want to write in an instruction if you have to, reminding yourself to slow down or 'look left' if there's someone in particular in the audience to acknowledge. Make yourself as familiar as you can with the material so that when the moment comes, you'll be comfortable looking up and away from the text rather than keeping your gaze fixed on it.

It should always be about the words rather than the voice, but if the voice fails, as Theresa May's did during her party conference speech in 2017, it can feel catastrophic. As she took to the stage that day she was already under pressure after the weak election result of a few months earlier, and she needed to use the moment to rally her party and show them she was a leader they could still believe in. But first afflicted by throat problems and then interrupted by a prankster, it got to the point where she could only get out a few words at a time and the dominant sound in the conference hall was of her cough, horribly amplified by the microphones. She had apparently been suffering from a cold all week, but as any broadcaster will know, a coughing fit can set in unexpectedly and when it does, a long text that needs to be delivered without any breaks is the worst possible prospect. What might have helped? Perhaps dropping the voice down almost to a whisper and letting the microphones do the work, and I know I'd have been sorely tempted to pull off the lapel microphone and turn away from the lectern to get the cough out rather than keep trying to suppress it.

In truth there were no good options available as she stood there in the full glare of the television cameras, struggling to deliver her lines. But why are speeches ever written at that sort of length, when they are hard to listen to as well as deliver? When I print out a speech and see it run to too many sides of A4 paper, alarm bells ring and I go back over it, working out what can be cut out or trimmed. Once I feel that everything remaining in the text deserves to be there, I break it down into very short paragraphs, separating some lines out entirely so they stand alone. Odd as this appears on paper, it helps to keep the pace measured and, in turn, keep the speech as close as possible to how you naturally sound, with added emphasis and flourish where necessary.

There is also a powerful potential effect from being willing to come to a complete halt. Like Christine Lagarde, it's something Elizabeth Butler-Sloss believes in: 'You have to be able to pause at the end of a sentence or paragraph and be brave about it,' she says, and for her that could mean thirty seconds or more – which, if you try it, is a considerable length of time and does indeed require a certain courage.

In broadcasting, knowing when to pause and how to vary your pace are essential techniques to master – especially in situations that are outside the normal everyday pattern. It might be when providing commentary for special events – weighing up when it is more appropriate to let music or other sound take over and hold your own words back – or when dealing with breaking news. Here, you have to guard against a tendency to rush, not only in order to strike the right tone but for practical reasons. If you are on air for an indefinite period with very little information, possibly just one line on an explosion or other incident, you need to take your time delivering it.

All of the above will apply to men as much as women, and in fact linguistics experts often warn against drawing conclusions about gender difference in this area. Professor Deborah Cameron of Oxford University dislikes generalisations about women's speech and wrote a 2007 book drawing on three decades of research conducted on language, communications and the sexes. 'The idea that men and women differ fundamentally in the way they use language to communicate is a myth in the everyday sense: a widespread but false belief', she wrote.[6] When women's speech *is* singled out for particular comment or analysis, she says it reveals a depressing lack of progress: 'This endless policing of women's language – their voices, their intonation patterns, the words they use, their syntax – is uncomfortably similar to the way our culture polices women's bodily appearance.'[7]

At an individual level, however, most of us will have an awareness of the habits of our own speech and probably a desire to change some of them. My own were brought home to me when the *Today* programme used a selection of my interviews to explore the capacity of artificial intelligence in terms of linguistic communication. The transcripts were fed into a bot developed by Sheffield University, which I then 'interviewed', recognising my own speech patterns – including how often I resort to 'right' and 'so' – in conversation.[8]

As someone who earns a living through speech, I am probably particularly conscious of my vocabulary and interested in ways of improving it, and there are phrases that I now try to guard against. When complimented on an interview my default response used to be to question or undermine the praise ('Do you think so? I'm not sure about that last question') or say that I had got lucky. Perhaps my background was playing a role. When I was growing up, compliments or praise would invariably have a phrase such as '*maashallah*' – by the Grace of God – attached to them rather than being all about individual achievement.

I started to think about this in a new way after realising how the questioning of positive feedback might appear from the perspective of a manager or senior colleague. My only experience of being at the hiring end of the recruitment process has been when looking for childcare, and one day it hit me: if someone I was thinking of employing was similarly doubtful about their abilities, perhaps saying, 'Yes, I *think* I can look after your sons', they would hardly inspire my confidence. The columnist and author India Knight has written about coming to a similar conclusion, after regularly responding to a compliment by mentioning a flaw of some kind. Finally, she decided she had to stop: 'Beyond a certain point, you simply can't stand there saying "This cake I made is disgusting", even as people are helping themselves to thirds. You start to sound unhinged.'[9]

Now, I try to make a simple 'thank you' my default response to a positive comment. In writing too, I am conscious of words and phrases that add doubt where it is not necessary. Rather than beginning an email with 'I just wondered' or 'Sorry to bother you', I try to open with something more neutral, perhaps 'I am writing to ask if you might consider'. The recipients may never notice the difference, but I feel I have begun on a positive rather than a diffident note.

The novelist Elizabeth Day made a similar change after writing a book in which her protagonist was an uncompromising self-made millionaire called Howard Pink.[10] 'When I began to find his voice,' she says, 'he sprung on to the page as unashamedly male and blessed with a defiant sense of his own entitlement.' As the book, *Paradise City*, progressed, she found that writing about Howard was having an effect on the way she expressed herself in real life: 'Some of his confidence began to leak into my daily interactions. I got sick of my hesitant email manner, especially when pitching ideas to my editors. I challenged myself to leave out those tiny mitigating words that simply served to undermine my own thoughts.'[11] At first her more direct emails felt almost rude, but often the response was positive. And even otherwise, they had a beneficial effect:

'When my emails languished unanswered or when my ideas were turned down, it no longer felt like a personal slight because I had invested less of my own tortuous emotional energy into the transaction.'

The writer and comedian Viv Groskop went as far as to turn the overuse of 'sorry' into the basis of a one-woman show, spurred by the 'pointless apologising' she says she saw around her and in herself. 'I took it as being a female thing because the more I noticed it in myself, the more I noticed it in other women.' She thinks it happens because women are stereotyped as those who smooth the way: 'It is women's role to be the appeaser, to bring in a maternal quality, to be unthreatening. That's why women do tend to couch things they say in meetings with "Sorry to mention this".'[12] Amy Schumer, who was once in a memorable sketch where a group of outstanding professional women keep apologising for increasingly absurd reasons, says she has also found herself doing it too much in real life: 'I'd be on set when we were filming *Trainwreck* and I would want to give a suggestion to Judd Apatow and I'd say "Sorry". And then I noticed and thought, what am I doing?'[13]

What is worth doing is thinking about the balance to be struck between having perfectly normal doubts about our abilities or ideas, and articulating them to the extent that they become embedded in our outward persona. Think of Eleanor Roosevelt – who came to prominence as the wife of an American president but went on to break the mould of what a first lady could be. She grew up with many uncertainties about herself and described her early married life as that of a conventional society matron. It was her husband's ill-health that pushed her into speaking and campaigning on his behalf. 'You must do the thing you think you cannot do,' she later said, and today she is remembered not only for her White House years but as one of the twentieth century's most influential Americans.

In Brief

Emphasis is what matters

Many people become unnecessarily self-conscious about their accent or pronunciation. Think instead about diction and emphasis – clarity and being understood by those listening to you is paramount. Often, what feels to you like over-emphasis will come out just fine to the listener; the danger of the other way is that maintaining what you think is a neutral tone ends up sounding flat.

Own your script

If you're delivering a speech, read it aloud or at the very least mouth the words in advance. Some sentences look fine written down, but when you come to speak them you discover that the punctuation or phrasing doesn't lend itself to a natural delivery. Make sure the words are ones you would normally use in speech, and once you have got the script right, practise it enough to make yourself completely familiar and comfortable with the content. If a gust of wind blew away your papers, you should be able to get by without them.

Don't be afraid to re-work and annotate

You might want to write instructions into your script, such as 'pause', 'look up' and 'slow down'. It can also help to break down the paragraphs so that some sentences stand alone, or to play with the written layout – if you centre your lines on the page, for instance, they can be easier to read at a glance.

Ditch the doubt and the apology

In everyday speech or emails, beware of default phrases that can convey doubt about your own abilities, or make you sound apologetic when you have no need to be.

Standing Up

Those with a deep understanding of human body language will always be in a better position to interpret the feelings, motives and machinations of others

Desmond Morris

There is a scene in Shakespeare's *Hamlet* in which the Prince turns director, instructing a group of players exactly how they are to deliver lines that are of the utmost importance, because they'll be used to observe the reactions of those he suspects of murder. He tells the actors not to overdo it and then adds: 'Be not too tame neither, but let your own discretion be your tutor. Suit the action to the word, the word to the action.' So too in television news – you don't want to distract the viewer with expansive and irritating gestures, but the presenter sitting statue-like and rigid will also appear odd.

In reality, life is full of non-verbal cues and gestures that add to the way we convey meaning: we might lean forward to listen more intently, lean back when we don't like what we hear, rise to greet someone who is important to us, or merely gesture them into a seat if they are less so. Body language is far more revealing than most of us realise and yet few of us give it the thought it deserves.

For those in public positions and followed by cameras nearly everywhere, non-verbal communication holds both peril and opportunity. From the start of Donald Trump's election campaign, for example, his extensive gesturing helped cultivate a distinctive image. Rather than the controlled demeanour most politicians would adopt at a podium – designed to underline statesman-like credentials – he would keep his arms moving and use his hands for emphasis, giving the impression of a man secure in himself and needing nothing. 'He comes across as incredibly confident,' says the communications expert and coach Mary Civiello. 'It's not just his hand gestures but his facial gestures. He addresses audiences of his supporters and so he feels completely free to speak in a very animated way. It's effective because it's dynamic. It's the way we are when we speak to friends and we don't have to worry about being cautious in what we say.'

She charts the contrast between two sets of Trump movements: big gestures and flailing arms to convey a sense of disorder in America and the world – and then controlled, pincer-like hands to emphasise how it would be fixed under him. 'He gets people whipped up with his gestures,' she explains. 'He gets them to feel a sense of chaos, and then he follows it up with precision moves:

"Elect me and we'll get to the bottom of this.'" Those smaller, tighter gestures, she says, send out the message that he is the one who can act in the face of the madness.[1]

Once in office, President Trump was seen in novel social situations – greeting world leaders and hosting gatherings at the White House. Suddenly, the unusual way he shook hands began to stand out: at the announcement of Neil Gorsuch as his choice for the Supreme Court, he appeared to jerk the judge towards him when shaking his hand. A few days later the Japanese Prime Minister Shinzo Abe was on the receiving end – the photocall after their talks involved his hand repeatedly patted and pulled closer by the president, and held for longer than seemed comfortable.

Was what was going on a conscious effort at dominance, an effort to signal who'd be calling the shots in the relationship? In those early days of the administration, only Justin Trudeau appeared to have mastered how to handle the new president's greeting style. Arriving at the White House, the Canadian prime minister took the initiative and moved forward to close the distance, putting his hand onto Donald Trump's upper arm as they shook hands.

The Stanford University professor Deborah Gruenfeld says there is often a power dynamic that can be observed in people's body language: those who have a higher status take up more physical space, while others tend to shrink themselves down, look away more and are also more likely to smile. 'It's not because things are better at the bottom,' she says. 'People in the lower ranks are smiling because it's their job to make sure people above them are never uncomfortable.'[2]

You need to be particularly aware of this dynamic, she suggests, if you're trying to convince or influence. 'Understand what is at stake and adjust. If you are saying something authoritative, stop smiling. On the other hand, if you sense someone is threatened by your competence, perhaps give them a smile.'[3] Mary Civiello warns, however, about how jarring it can be when your words and your facial expressions are out of sync, using the example of a television interview given by the US education secretary Betsy DeVos. Throughout a series of tough questions over school policy, she kept smiling, but doing so made her appear out of touch with the seriousness of the subject.[4]

An early effort to quantify the role that body language plays in the messages we send came from Professor Albert Mehrabian in his 1971 book *Silent Messages*. In what he called a 'speech oriented culture', he said not enough attention was paid to the contribution of non-verbal behaviour to the process of communication. And yet, when we watch someone from afar, we will often make judgements: 'We can observe a stranger talking to others in a distant group without being able to hear his words, and we can feel we like or dislike or feel that we know the kind of person he is.'[5]

His analysis broke down the different ways in which we infer emotion in others: 55 per cent comes from facial expressions, 38 per cent from tone of voice and just 7 per cent from the words themselves. This means that if, for example, your words are polite but your tone of voice and facial expression are hostile, the overwhelming message will be negative. Professor Mehrabian used the example of a job interview: 'The applicant may say all the right things, but his contradictory behaviour may cost him the job … the interviewer may find that his bland and expressionless face and voice do little to confirm this verbalized enthusiasm, and may intuitively decide that he does not really mean what he says.'[6]

What accounts for the much greater power of non-verbal messages over others in the Mehrabian analysis? He believes that while most of us are taught that politeness may mean having to bite your tongue, we are not taught about body language. 'The continued emphasis on language skills both at home and in school,' he says, 'is a sharp contrast to the neglect of training in nonverbal communication.'[7] It's certainly true that I have thought much more over the years about the content of my scripts than about how I will sit or stand in the studio, while being quick to reach conclusions about other people based on their gestures or stance. It might be the way some people choose to remain standing in meetings – thus giving the impression that their time is too precious to devote much of it to a particular gathering – or the way senior figures, usually men, tend to make the most expansive use of office space. In some cities, 'manspreading' has led to signs going up on public transport: on buses in Madrid and on the subway in New York.[8]

Perhaps we haven't fully shaken off the age-old differences in the ways men and women have been schooled to occupy space. In an influential 1980 essay, the political scientist Iris Marion Young explored fellow researchers' analysis that femininity explains why a five-year-old girl throws a ball with less force and power than a boy of the same age. While Professor Young observed that a woman might approach a lifting task by bending down and focusing on using her arms – in contrast to a man planting himself firmly on the ground and using the power in his legs – she said the differences were not about anatomy or physiology, but socialisation: 'For the most part, girls and women are not given the opportunity to use their full bodily capacities in free and open engagement with the world, nor are they encouraged as much as boys to develop specific bodily skills,' she wrote.[9]

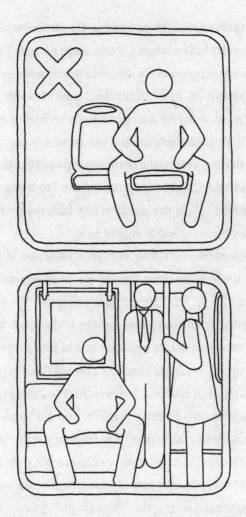

We are in a changed era today in terms of women's participation in sport at all levels, the emphasis on strength and fitness and the level of interest in watching women compete at the elite level. But there are still ways in which physical spaces are organised primarily with men in mind. I've lost track of the number of conference stages I've been on where bar stools are the chosen style of seating, giving an impression of informality but unfavourable if not downright awkward for women in heels or skirts. Lecterns, too, are often set at heights that suit men, leaving women speakers peering over the top, the microphone hiding their faces. And television news programmes often put a male presenter on the left, the position in which the eyes of the viewer most commonly first alight.

In some conservative or religious societies, it can be hard for women who are navigating professional life to figure out how to greet men in the workplace, in order to come across as an equal and set the right tone. What if shaking hands with the opposite sex is inappropriate or frowned upon? It can be hard to know what to do instead, as I have found in several countries. I try to be as purposeful as possible with a strong verbal acknowledgement and a nod of the head. There may be local customs that you can adopt: in North Africa, I saw people bringing their right hands over their hearts and dipping their heads in greeting, and followed suit.

Sometimes men have an advantage in appearing commanding simply because larger frames fill more of the available space – I feel this when working in large studios where there are swooping cameras and impressive angles but where it is easy to feel dwarfed by it all if you are on the smaller side. When Mary Civiello works with women in business, she advises them to think about how they can make small changes in how they use the space around them: 'I would never want women to try to be manly, but there are things that we can do that both men and women recognise as leadership communication. If you sit at a conference table and it's your moment to speak, don't crunch yourself up. Lean forward, widen your arms and take up a little more space. Look to the far right, the far left and straight down the room.' One woman she worked with reported that when she did this, she noticed that her audiences began paying more attention. 'She started to then feel more confident in real time.'

When it comes to first impressions, we know from a series of psychological studies how little time it takes for people to form judgements about one another – just a tenth of a second according to a 2006 study.[10] Another piece of research, based on videos of graduate teaching fellows at a university, found that a series of very short clips, played without sound to participants in an experiment, were strikingly similar to real-life assessments of the lecturers by their students.[11]

The study's main author, Nalini Ambady, said there was a wealth of information contained in these 'thin slices' of behaviour, underlining the importance of non-verbal cues in the formation of judgements. The teachers who fared less well in the evaluations tended to frown, fidget, look down or fiddle with an object such as a pen or a piece of chalk. The researchers also found a correlation between the teachers' perceived physical attractiveness and their perceived professional abilities, but even after this was controlled for, the overlap between the end-of-semester ratings and the ones based on a few seconds' impression remained high.

Malcolm Gladwell, who wrote a book called *Blink* about conclusions reached in the blink of an eye, says thin-slicing – or finding meaning from what is experienced in a short period of time – is essential for our unconscious to understand what is happening around us. 'It is a central part of what it means to be human. We thin-slice whenever we meet a new person or have to make sense of something quickly or encounter a novel situation. We thin-slice because we have to, and we come to rely on that ability because there are lots of situations where careful attention to the details of a very thin slice, even for no more than a second or two, can tell us an awful lot.'[12] In some ways this is pretty chilling, but it also reinforces Professor Mehrabian's argument for understanding the power of non-verbal as well as verbal communication.

Talking to colleagues about this revealed some of their own rituals. Kamal Ahmed, the BBC's editorial director, says that when waiting for an important meeting, he will never take the seat offered by the receptionist. 'When you sit down, your body relaxes and you lose focus, but if you stand you are more ready to present yourself. You are literally thinking on your feet.' One chief executive kept him waiting for twenty minutes, but he stood for the entire period because he wanted to greet him from that upright position. For him, there's a psychological advantage in the approach, which he says was particularly important at earlier stages of his career: 'Once people know more of your work, you naturally have more confidence and more presence. It's more important when you are going up the ladder.'

His words got me thinking: in the waiting-room situation he described, I would probably take advantage of the offered seat, and then, most likely, take out my phone and use the time to catch up with emails, news or social media. That would in turn mean that when the person I was waiting for appeared, they would find me looking down, shoulders hunched, engrossed in something other than the forthcoming meeting. I'd be unlikely to make the best possible first impression.

In some professions, posture is not only about the image you project but also goes to the heart of what you can achieve; if teachers do not command attention they cannot enable the learning of their pupils. Jo Palmer-Tweed, who runs a teacher training college, says body language is an implicit part of learning to be an effective teacher. 'Once you set yourself at the front of the room you have put yourself in a position of extreme authority. The message to the children is that you know the answers. You need to maintain that authority while also being in amongst the learners. If you are giving out non-verbal signals that you are anxious, your class will be anxious and that's not what you want in education.'

As women teachers can face being pigeonholed in a maternal role, she encourages them to establish themselves as nurturing figures rather than taking on a parenting-style approach. And for both men and women, body language will be an essential tool in managing classroom behaviour, often cited as one of the greatest fears for newer teachers. 'The way you walk through the door, the type of eye contact you make with pupils in those first few seconds can make or break a lesson,' she says. Experienced teachers will have got to the point where this comes naturally, but for those early in their careers she suggests they psych themselves up in advance: 'I'm going to walk into this room, the children are going to look at me, and they're going to be quiet and listen because I've got something important to say.'[13]

In 2012, one psyching-up technique that caught on fast came from a TED talk by the psychologist Amy Cuddy.

She used her research on the effect of 'high power poses' – sitting or standing in expansive positions – to suggest that they could be used to help people feel more powerful before a big or stressful moment in their lives.[14] One pose in particular caught on: legs apart, hands on hips in the style of Wonder Woman. Amy Cuddy was later criticised because the physiological effects on hormone levels that she and her co-author had reported in their original work could not be replicated. But Mary Civiello is in no doubt about the individual value of deploying these techniques. 'There is no question that the psychology of being bigger or acting bigger works. It stands to reason – before singers and performers go out onto a stage they don't sit hunched up, they move around.' For some, the techniques may be so simple they barely think about it: taking a deep breath, standing up tall, or in my case, waving my arms about and stretching to get the blood flowing before going into the studio.

At other times our bodies betray us and send the opposite message to the one we would give if we had thought about it: the wandering gaze that reveals a lack of interest or attention, the look that shifts quickly to someone else in the room, or – closest to home for me – checking my phone. I know that when I do this in front of my children, the message of my words ('It's work … just give me a minute') will be entirely contradicted and overridden by that of my actions: what I am really telling them is that something else is more compelling to me at that moment than they are. How easy it is to judge others harshly when they do this: how much harder to face up to our own choices.

In Brief

Be aware of non-verbal power

This is especially the case when your words are conveying one message but your body language suggests something different, such as if you appear shifty, avoid eye contact or otherwise send a contradictory message. Maintain a consistency between the two.

Be expansive in how you occupy space

Don't shrink yourself down into a chair or place yourself in the corner of a room. Lean forward or use your arms to fill more of the space around you. You have a right to be there.

Think about standing

Teachers do this to command attention, and in a public-speaking scenario I would always choose to deliver at least part of what I say from a standing position. It conveys a sense of confidence and of readiness.

Choose a way to physically psych yourself up

It may be breathing, a particular exercise or a routine, but once you have established what helps you look and feel the part, deploy it before you walk into the room – or from the moment you rise to your feet and take the floor for whatever reason. Think of the way actors inhabit their character from before they step onto the stage and maintain it until after they are in the wings – the same applies to you.

The Digital You

The internet is the organising
principle of our age

Martha Lane Fox

Instagram, Facebook, Twitter, LinkedIn – like body language, what we say and share on social media is revealing of our interests, priorities or personalities. Too revealing at times, as has been discovered by people taking on new roles and discovering that a trawl through their online footprint paints a picture that is less than flattering. In 2017, the new editor of the *Gay Times* was sacked soon after being appointed, when his Twitter history was shown to include deeply offensive posts.[1] A few months earlier, the Labour Party candidate for the parliamentary seat of Stoke-on-Trent had to apologise when a trawl back through his Twitter feed revealed a series of disparaging posts about women, including referring to one as a 'polished turd'.[2] They all dated from before he ran for Parliament, and he still became an MP, but it was a terrible start to a career as an elected representative of the people.

When I see a critical response on Twitter to something I have said on air, I will often scroll down that person's feed to try to get a sense of them and their view; they may just turn out to be an expert in the area I have been discussing. Whatever the platform, there will be conclusions you reach based on the content someone chooses to post, how often they do so and how much they share about their lives – my view of one fellow journalist was forever altered by their gym selfies. Sometimes you wonder about taste and decency – or the lack of it. At the memorial to 9/11 victims at Ground Zero, I watched other visitors take selfies by the voids and couldn't understand the need to put yourself in the picture at a place that marks a mass murder.

All sorts of patterns can emerge when a social media feed is analysed in detail and over a period of time. When the writer Kate Imbach looked at 470 photographs posted on Melania Trump's Twitter feed between 2012 and 2015, she noticed how often the future First Lady appeared to be walking behind her husband and son. Sometimes they would be in the front seats of a car while she was in the back, or they would be walking together up the steps of a plane as she followed. There were also regular pictures of the view from high up in Trump Tower or the windows of a plane, looking down on the world. 'She lives behind glass,' concluded Imbach, noting that even the pictures of Central Park or of sightseeing trips in Washington DC and

Barcelona, all appeared to be taken from inside cars. 'Her idea of a walk in the park is a drive.'[3]

Despite the dark side of social media in the form of trolling and hate, the digital world is one of huge possibility and enrichment. I know that I am a better journalist thanks to the range of easily accessible information sources, and more connected to audiences thanks to the availability of instant reaction. I have seen how the internet has been an outlet for news which would otherwise never have travelled – in Tunisia in 2011, young men in the small town of Sidi Bouzid told me how they put mobile phone footage of anti-government protests onto Facebook. They'd been out on the streets demonstrating in the wake of the death of an impoverished young fruit seller, but state media would never have broadcast evidence of such anger. It was thanks to social media that the protests spread.

In Egypt, one activist told me that when he saw how the Tunisian president had been toppled, he was determined to try to achieve the same in his own country. In Libya, a man who'd filmed a crowd tearing down a stone monument to Gaddafi in Tobruk raced to upload the pictures from an internet cafe, knowing access would soon be cut off. Only when he saw his footage broadcast on Arab satellite TV channels the following day did he know it had made it through.

Each platform has its own nuances in how it might be used: for me Twitter is for work, Facebook mostly for keeping in touch with far-flung family and friends, Instagram for visual pleasures and the sights that lift my heart. I can see how LinkedIn is skilfully used to enhance and develop professional reputations, not only keeping a CV updated and always available, but with the endorsements from colleagues and former colleagues that add weight and credibility to an employment history.

Almost every day on Twitter I see people with particular expertise or knowledge using the platform to demonstrate it and add to the understanding of others. It might be an academic who's seen their subject crop up on the news or a misconception circulate and decide to address it, sometimes through a thread or series of linked tweets. Often their views are picked up and quoted by journalists, amplifying their audience. Or it might be someone who has a specific insight into a situation that's the subject of debate, perhaps because they were there or they know the key people involved. Again, they might thread posts together to tell a fuller story, perhaps laying out their credentials right at the start: 'I worked at that charity in 2017 and this is what I saw.'

For some people, the digital projection of themselves is transformative, allowing an interest or passion to become a career. Zoella was nineteen when she started to become known as a blogger and YouTuber, going on to develop a cult following for videos on everything from beauty products to anxiety. Izy Hossack was even younger – seventeen – when her Instagram baking pictures attracted attention and a book deal. For Jack Monroe, it was recipes devised as a single parent on a tight budget that led to a book deal and a career as a writer and campaigner.

Initiatives launched by women often stand out in the world of online campaigning, according to Jennifer Dulski, president of the petition website Change.org. 'Women are really good at telling their personal stories and the campaigns we see as most successful on the site are the ones where people really explain why the issue matters to them and sometimes are willing to be vulnerable about the way they describe that,' she says. 'They also share with their networks in a more effective way and have a certain amount of persistence where they aren't as willing to let the campaigns close.'[4] One such was Laura Coryton's petition against sanitary products being subject to taxes, which she contrasted with exemptions for helicopters and alcoholic jellies.[5] And it was three women – Alicia Garza, Patrisse Khan-Cullors and Opal Tometi – who used the hashtag #BlackLivesMatter after the man who shot dead unarmed black teenager Trayvon Martin was found not guilty of murder. Together they provided an outlet for the outrage felt at that time and now #BlackLivesMatter is a focal point for people to share their own experiences of racism, profiling and policing.

The first rule for building an effective individual presence on social media is to be consistent: deciding what you will blog, post or tweet about, doing it regularly and developing a coherent digital identity in the process. There will be choices to make about whether it will be a purely professional exercise or something more personal. But even if it's the latter, it's worth thinking through how open you should sensibly be. However empowering it may feel to have your say on a given topic, how much do you really want your colleagues, bosses or *future* colleagues and bosses to know about you? All of us are likely to have multiple groups of people in our lives who matter to us in different ways: relatives and friends but also colleagues and neighbours, perhaps pupils or the teachers of our children. In the real world our conversations would vary in tone and content between these individuals and groups but that subtlety is unavailable in a social media feed.

For those developing a brand, the platforms can be fantastic promotional tools that are also capable of conveying a sense of the person behind the product or service. I love seeing how my make-up artist friend Louise Heywood uses Instagram and Facebook to take people behind the scenes of her work, sharing images of the tools of her trade and before and after shots of her subjects, as well as product reviews that come with the credibility that she knows what she is talking about. For those working in – or trying to get into – industries where LinkedIn is relied upon, a well-thought-out, well-presented profile is a valuable shop window. Not only can your CV be easily accessible but endorsements from past colleagues add credibility and sharing some well-thought-out work-related posts or articles will personalise the content. Try to imagine a recruiter or prospective employer looking you up there: you would want everything they see about you to be sharp, and in line with your professional direction.

For those in senior or high-profile positions, not being plugged into social media means they may be one step removed from seeing how public sentiment is shifting or a story or campaign that might affect them is going viral. When a United Airlines passenger was filmed being dragged off an overbooked plane in 2017, suffering considerable injury in the process, the video was shared instantly around the world, sparking outrage. But the first statement from the airline's chief executive Oscar Munoz did not mention the use of force, referring instead to having to 're-accommodate' passengers and how the incident was 'upsetting to all at United'. In an email to staff, he referred to the injured passenger as 'disruptive and belligerent'. But as the uproar continued, and United's share price dropped, his statements changed, until he admitted in a television interview that the airline had got its response badly wrong.[6] He and his top team might have made different judgements had they been better tuned in to the online reaction from the outset and gauged how the damage was multiplying with every share of the footage.

One person who has seen the entire trajectory of the internet's development and its effect on our lives is Martha Lane Fox. She was twenty-five when she co-founded lastminute.com in 1998, persuading investors that there was money to be made in this strange new area called e-commerce. But that is a rare example of a tech company associated with a woman – elsewhere in this young industry, which has created so many cutting-edge products, the roll call of founders is almost all male: Sergey Brin and Larry Page of Google, Jeff Bezos of Amazon, Mark Zuckerberg of Facebook, Jack Dorsey of Twitter, Jack Ma of Alibaba, Travis Kalanick of Uber, Kevin Systrom and Mike Krieger of Instagram.

Women are scarce, too, in decision-making roles in private equity and venture capital firms, which have the power to give some ideas the chance to blossom while killing others dead. When Natalie Massenet, founder of Net-a-Porter, looked back on how hard it was in the late 1990s to win support for the fashion website, she noted how much incomprehension she encountered: 'There were a lot of unimaginative private equity people who said that women would never shop online. I think about those people a lot. I'm sure their wives are having Net-a-Porter bags delivered to their homes every day.' A decade after it launched, her company was valued at more than $500 million.[7]

Today 68 per cent of Google employees around the world are men,[8] while Facebook is 63 per cent male, rising to 77 per cent in technical roles.[9] While there is clearly an issue with finding and hiring qualified female software engineers, the culture in some companies has also been blamed for driving them out. When site reliability engineer (SRE) Susan Fowler wrote about what she called her 'very, very strange year at Uber', she said she witnessed many women leaving the company, partly because of its lack of organisation but also because of sexism. By the time she departed in December 2016, the 150-strong team of SREs was down to just 3 per cent women.[10]

Martha Lane Fox says this female deficit will have far-reaching implications – for the companies, society, and women themselves. 'Anyone who's ever run a business knows that the person who can code the stuff rules the world – the ones who can fix a website or get rid of a bug are driving everything from better customer experience to better interaction with the government.' These are also the jobs of the future, which is why a failure to address the numbers of women in them might mean gender pay gaps end up being exacerbated rather than reduced. 'This is a sector that is becoming more and more important to all of us, but we are biasing rapidly growing businesses, money creation and high-paid jobs against women. We cannot be absent from this new world or we will end up again in lower-paid jobs.'

Parts of the tech industry are now coming up with their own ideas about how to encourage more women into science, technology and mathematics. One Swedish-based company, Semcon, has designed a search engine modification that gender-balances image searches, an idea sparked by the make-up of its own workforce. 'To make the best products, we need to put people's needs and behaviours first, and since half of the world's population is female, we need more women choosing to become engineers. Without role models, we may not get there,' it says. Once you download its browser extension 'Re-Search', a search for 'engineer' produces a series of images of women as well as the standard set dominated by male faces. Other professions in the industry – software developer, game designer – are also included, as are occupations beyond, including some where the imbalance is the other way around – a search on 'childminder' pulls up a set of pictures dominated by men with children.[11]

Image searches may seem relatively innocuous, but what if an algorithm similar to the one that throws up almost exclusively male software developers is used in recruitment, or in finding speakers for conferences or experts to give media comment? You might hope – or assume – that the system understands that the correlation of 'female' with 'sister' or 'princess' is not the same as between 'female' and 'teacher'. But when one group of researchers tested a common machine learning algorithm by asking it to complete the phrase 'Man is to Computer Programmer as Woman is to X', the answer that came back for 'X' was 'Homemaker'. It was not that the system was inaccurate, it understood well that 'he' referred to a brother and 'she' to a sister, but it also thought that 'he' corresponded to 'doctor' and 'she' to 'nurse', as well as 'he' to 'architect' and 'she' to 'interior designer'.[12]

Any data set is only as good as the information fed into it in the first place, its predictions based on associations and patterns discernible in the world around us. A bias within the data will be reflected in the results it produces, which is why the Harvard professor Barbara Grosz, who developed some of the earliest language processing and computer dialogue systems, believes that ethics must be part of product design from the start. Without this, machine learning algorithms are likely to magnify the existing imbalances. 'It's not that you can avoid all kinds of bias,' she says, 'but developers of AI systems need to be mindful in their design, and careful about what they claim about their programmes and their results.'[13]

As users, we should also be mindful that however expansive and international the internet might appear, what we find online reflects the geography of power. For all the wealth of information in the millions of pages on Wikipedia, the editors who contribute to it are not only overwhelmingly male but also mostly based in Europe and North America. Articles will, naturally, reflect their world-view, as has been acknowledged by the site's founder Jimmy Wales: 'Our community has traditionally come from the tech and computer geek world and as we know that's very male-dominated. Our editors, who write what they're passionate and knowledgeable about, don't have a completely diverse set of things that they're interested in.' One example came on the day of Prince William's marriage to Catherine Middleton in 2011. As the bride appeared, a page was created about her dress – a garment of historical importance as the wedding dress of a future Queen. But it sparked a fierce row, as editors who regarded the subject matter as trivial tried to have the page deleted.

Today's online encyclopedia is tomorrow's historical record, and while ours is a hyper-connected age, some stories and experiences stand a much better chance than others of being noticed, celebrated and saved for posterity.

When Anasuya Sengupta co-founded the Whose Knowledge? campaign, she was motivated by wanting to see Africa, Asia and Latin America – where most of the world's population live – much better represented on the internet. The very first Wikipedia article she wrote was about a prominent British Nigerian, Bisi Adeleye-Fayemi, the co-founder of the African Women's Development Fund, after Sengupta spotted that she did not have her own page. Considering that the key test – for the person to be worthy of notice – had been met, she gathered biographical details and sources and published. But like the wedding dress, this page was also soon flagged for deletion, with other editors rejecting the premise that its subject was noteworthy. 'Unfortunately, very few Wikipedians look like me,' concluded Sengupta. 'Brown, female, and from the global South.'[14]

Now, her organisation works to help marginalised communities such as India's Dalits bring their knowledge online, or Native American groups to put their forefathers' experience into Wikipedia articles about the American gold rush. With women still making up only around 17 per cent of Wikipedia biographies, it's also run a campaign called #VisibleWikiWomen to add more photographs and images of notable female figures to the site, while the BBC's '100 Women' initiative has hosted global Wikipedia edit-a-thons, adding hundreds of new profiles.[15]

Martha Lane Fox hopes that the next stage of the internet is for it to act as a public good, transforming every aspect of our lives. 'The way we think about education, caring for the elderly, mental health, the end of life. Yet so many people making decisions in these areas feel wildly ill-equipped to understand what is possible.' Should everyone therefore be learning to code? 'Arguably over the next fifty years robots will be doing the coding for us. But over the next twenty years we are still going to need coders and if you know how to do it you will have the confidence and the capacity to have the conversation in a way that is more valuable. It's about problem-solving: seeing something that isn't working well for your group of friends or your family and thinking what the code solution to that might be.'

The problem many people would like to see solved is trolling and hate, not least because, in the words of the MP Yvette Cooper, no one wants it to be 'the new normal for the digital generation'. 'We work, rest and play online,' she says. 'That's why it is so damaging if some voices are drowned out, or if some people feel forced offline by threats or targeted abuse.'[16] In the case of Gina Miller, the abuse she received after leading legal challenges to the government included death threats. 'I expected people to be nasty,' she said. 'I didn't expect people to say I wasn't even human, that I was a primate, and that I should be beheaded and shot.'[17] One man was later jailed for offering a financial reward on Facebook to someone prepared to run her over.

Twitter can also be an unpleasant place for high-profile women. In the run-up to the 2017 general election, female MPs from ethnic minorities were more likely to be the recipients of abusive tweets than their white peers. And for any individuals who find themselves at the centre of an online storm it can be a humiliating as well as a frightening experience. In December 2013, a thirty-year-old public relations executive called Justine Sacco sent a joke tweet to her 170 Twitter followers just before she boarded a plane to South Africa: 'Going to Africa. Hope I don't get AIDS. Just kidding. I'm white!' With her phone off, she had no idea until she landed, many hours later, that her words had spread far and wide and turned her into a hate figure. She was called a racist and ended up losing her job. When she later talked to the writer Jon Ronson, it was clear that she never thought anyone would take her words literally or that she would be subjected to such intense and disproportionate vitriol. With her name known for all the wrong reasons, she found it hard to be employed again and there was a searing effect on her personal life too: 'I'm single, so it's not like I can date, because we Google everyone we might date. That's been taken away from me too.'[18]

What, if anything, can help if you find yourself the target of online hate? The journalist Barkha Dutt, whose work has made her one of India's most prominent public figures, with a Twitter following in the millions, has repeatedly been in that position. She's been called a 'presstitute', threatened with violence, seen stories emerge about fictitious husbands, been labelled a traitor to her country and even accused of fabricating the sexual abuse she suffered as an eight-year-old.[19] Having done everything from ignoring the nasties to outing them, from taking part in anti-trolling campaigns to filing criminal complaints, she says she now barely notices it: 'That's how dangerously inured I have become to the gross innuendo and violent and sexually explicit abuse that is heaped on so many women.'

I asked Martha Lane Fox how she felt about the connected world that she experienced as an internet pioneer being a place in which people can encounter so much hostility. 'The internet is a reflection of the real world but it amplifies and enables the worst of the mob mentality because it combines it with apparent anonymity,' she says. 'Before it, if you were a mean, horrible person who liked being shouty about women, you may have had a couple of friends you could do it with, or maybe a weird magazine, but there wasn't the ability to quickly find other people with similar feelings.' She reminds me that the online world is still in its early days and has the potential to develop for the better. 'We do need to be more demanding of these platforms,' she says. 'You can, through product design, make huge shifts in how people talk to each other.'

It feels as though the tech companies are more alive to this than they used to be – from time to time pressure builds and we see new initiatives launched and new reporting tools become available. We also know more about the manufacture of trolling. In late 2017, a US congressional committee released details of social media content linked to Russia-based troll factories, including a long list of Twitter accounts suspended on that basis. With most, it would have been impossible to tell that they were not as they appeared. They included photos of the supposed account holder, and what appeared to be personal details. To me, it was the moment that first brought home what is possible with industrial-scale trolling and the pumping out of poisonous material. It doesn't mean there aren't also hateful individuals out there. But there may not be quite as many as you think.[20]

In Brief

Develop a coherent social media identity

Are your feeds just for family and friends? If so they should probably be private. If not, they are part of a public profile and your followers won't always know you personally. Consider how you want to portray yourself – what impression will strangers form of your interests, attitudes and passions from scrolling through your posts? Once you have worked out that the sense you are projecting of yourself is the one you want, be consistent and stick to your chosen style or theme.

A shop window for your skills

Your digital self can be a valuable showcase either for the breadth of your knowledge about your existing field or as a way of illustrating something else that you enjoy. Tweets about books or food or tech might turn into a good sideline, perhaps even a new line of work, or at the very least show colleagues and acquaintances a lesser-known and interesting side of you.

Pause before you post

Almost everyone gets burned on social media at some point, but a few basic ground rules can help guard against the graver or career-limiting end of the spectrum of potential pitfalls. As a matter of course, get into the habit of taking a quick glance back at your words before they're sent out into the world. For anything particularly complex or controversial, draft something and let it sit for a few moments before looking at it again – or consider asking someone else to cast a quick eye over it.

Trolling – respond or rise above?

This is a judgement call that will depend on the nature of the comment as well as your own threshold for contention and conflict. But consider also whether engaging at length is worth your energies. Even if you 'win', you may look back and feel it was time you'll never get back.

Keeping Sharp

Fright can transform into petrol

Judi Dench

Back in the real, physical world, there is a question that I was regularly asked which had the capacity to tie me up in knots every single time. It was a simple and courteous one: did I enjoy presenting *Today*? For the first few years I appeared on the programme, I struggled to answer, unable to associate the word 'enjoy' with it. From the tight knot in my stomach the night before a shift, as I worried about and tried to anticipate what I would find on my desk at four the next morning, to the pressure of getting to grips with a large amount of information in a short time, the overall picture felt very far from enjoyment.

Gradually, the experience shifted, becoming closer to anticipation than fear. I seemed to have more ability to channel my nerves and was able to ride the ups and downs of the programme with greater equanimity. Then, one day, when asked the same question about whether I was enjoying it, I was able to answer in the affirmative – not every moment of every day on air, and certainly not when things go wrong, but for the most part, *yes*.

Two things made the difference. The first was simply familiarity: the more times I did the job, the more I learned and the more comfortable I felt. Practice did not – and should not – make perfect, if such a state even exists, but it did aid performance. It's easy to look back now and think that that degree of greater comfort would always have come, but in my early days in a highly scrutinised role, it did not feel that way. Had I only been assigned to the programme for a time-limited period, I might also never have got to the point at which I felt more at ease. I might have left thinking that the apprehension I felt meant I was unsuited to it or not up to the challenge. And while the importance of practice in sport and music is widely recognised, we often seem to look at performance in other areas and imagine that individuals had that ability from the get-go.

In reality, they will have learned from each task, project, patient, flight, challenge, or – in my industry – broadcast. They will have put in the hours, including in the disciplines which may at first glance appear to hinge on artistic brilliance. The composer John Williams, who has scored more than a hundred films in fifty years in the business, says most people have 'romantic notions' about the process of creativity: 'Any working composer or painter or sculptor will tell you that inspiration comes at the eighth hour of labour, rather than as a bolt out of the blue.'[1] And while practice in itself is no guarantee of success, the writer and former sportsman Matthew Syed says it has a value not only in aiding mastery of a particular task, but reducing the likelihood of seizing up, or 'choking', at a high-pressure moment. 'In order to overcome choking we must trust our subconscious competence,' he says. 'It turns out that we are far more likely to do so when we are as familiar as possible with the situation we are about to face.'[2]

The second shift that occurred for me was being able to recognise that the nervousness I felt – and still feel, albeit to a more manageable extent – was not only normal but necessary. It acts like a wake-up call, giving me the jolt I need to remind me that I must find the right bit of information or formulate the best possible question *now*. It focuses my mind and harnesses my energies.

Dame Judi Dench, widely regarded as one of the best actors of her generation, has said that fear is always part of her professional life: 'I get stage fright all the time; the more I act, the more I feel it. But you just have to use it to your advantage. Fear engenders a huge amount of energy and you have to make it work for the better, otherwise you'd crumble.'[3] Her phrase about fright turning into petrol rings true with me, most often when I sit down to do a pre-recorded interview and have to work hard to try and summon the buzz that is naturally there with a live programme.

Judi Dench is not the only actor of her calibre to feel this way. For one of her peers, Dame Maggie Smith, worries about new roles have grown rather than receded with her years in acting. 'When you're young you're just so thrilled to be doing it,' she said in 2015. 'As you get older you realise how difficult it is to do. When you're young, it's excitement and terror. Now it's just terror.'[4]

For Eleanor Roosevelt, the key to conquering fear was building up a series of successful experiences. 'You gain strength, courage and confidence by every experience in which you really stop to look fear in the face,' she said. 'You are able to say to yourself, "I have lived through this horror. I can take the next thing that comes along."'[5] In early life, her self-esteem was deeply affected by having a mother who was, she later wrote, 'troubled by my lack of beauty. She tried hard to bring me up well so that my manners would compensate for my looks, but her efforts only made me more keenly conscious of my shortcomings.'[6] The First World War proved to be a turning point, or her 'emancipation and education', as she put it, through her Red Cross work with wounded and recuperating soldiers.

If only it were possible to get that body of experience under your belt while ever so slightly under the radar, only then emerging into the spotlight. It doesn't work that way of course. When I spoke to the barrister Dinah Rose QC about her work, on cases ranging from employment and human rights to constitutional matters and competition law, she was quick to describe the fear that she felt as a younger lawyer: 'Advocacy is, objectively, completely terrifying. Everybody is putting the stress on you, everything hangs on what you do. If you're cross-examining a witness, it is a battle of wits between you, and if it gets out of control, it can be a catastrophe.'

She found the process so daunting when she started out that she used to throw up before going into court. But she now sees that period as a rite of passage. 'When you start out you are terrified, and you have to expect to be terrified. It's the same for every single person who starts at the Bar, and if they say otherwise they are lying to you.'

Now, when she stands up before a judge, she says she feels no fear. 'Experience makes it so much easier. Once you do something every day, it's your job, your routine. You learn how much time you have and how much preparation you need to do to feel comfortable,' she told me. 'And when you know these things, you gain confidence in your abilities. You have to have faith that it will stop being terrifying if you keep doing it.'

The detail of the routine she has established for herself in preparing for those court appearances plays a key role, just as my own early morning rituals help me. 'What I normally do is read all the factual documents first, then the case law or legal documents. I make notes and end up with one document that has all the relevant points of fact and another with all the relevant points of law,' she told me. 'The next most important thing is the structure. In what order will I make the points? How will I take the judge through the relevant cases? There are different ways you can present an argument that will make it more or less persuasive.' On the day of the hearing, she will rise early to script her opening argument. 'I've got four or five hours to get it down and the first part of the argument is really important because it needs to make the court focus.'

The rest of what she says will not be scripted, but her established method allows her to find what she needs quickly, under the pressure of questioning: 'It's all about preparation and structure. That gives you a route map.'[7] There are significant parallels between her world and mine, particularly in the need to communicate clearly, but the basic principle should resonate everywhere: you need to be in command of your subject, project or brief and that matters more than ever when you come up against a stress-ful moment.

In all of this, there is the question of degree – the amount of anxiety or fear that is to be expected and even helpful for a performance, and that which can be debilitating.

What is often talked about as the 'fight or flight' response dates back to the work of the American physiologist Dr Walter Bradford Cannon, who studied physiological changes in animals when they were startled or frightened by a perceived threat. A body of academic work built up, focusing on the release of hormones – especially adrenaline – their mobilising effect in acute or emergency situations, and the relationship between arousal of the body and performance levels.

It was the psychologists Robert Yerkes and John Dodson who put forward a theory about the effect of the degree of arousal, using the results of their experiments with mice. They said that stimulation – which in their experiment meant an electric shock – aided proficiency at a difficult task but only up to a certain point. If that stimulation became too intense, performance levels tailed off.[8] The idea became known as the Yerkes–Dodson Law, most often depicted on a graph as an upside-down 'U' – performance increases in line with arousal and then declines.

Ever since, the sweet spot in which the body is jerked out of its resting state but not pushed too far, has been fiercely sought after, and for obvious reasons. For Professor David Barlow, founder of the Center for Anxiety and Related Disorders at Boston University, it is not only personal development that is at stake, but human development in its widest sense. Without anxiety, little would be accomplished,' he writes. 'The performance of athletes, entertainers, executives, artisans, and students would suffer; creativity would diminish; crops might not be planted.'[9] But we also know the cost to individuals and society when it goes too far – one UK estimate said as many as 12.5 million working days were lost to work-related stress, depression or anxiety between 2016 and 2017.[10]

For some people anxiety will be extreme and disabling, disrupting everyday life and causing them to avoid certain situations. Others might find themselves experiencing panic attacks at particular moments. In these circumstances, the right professional help should make a difference. But there are also approaches that can help any of us with anxiety-inducing moments, and for me the security of a tried-and-tested working process is invaluable. It means that when I look at a brief that appears impenetrable, or have an important interview come up at short notice, I try to keep focused on the mechanics of what needs to be done next. That might mean concentrating on breaking down the text before me into headlines or bullet points; writing just the next script rather than worrying about all those to follow; or honing the first question for an interview rather than thinking about the entire sequence.

Caitlin Moran calls this doing the calm, right thing that is needed just for the next minute. In a heartfelt open letter to the girls who approached her at book signings, and who often seemed to be struggling with life, she wrote: 'However much it feels like you're approaching an event, an exam, a conversation, a decision, a kiss, where if you screw up the entire future will just burn to hell in front of you and you will end, you are not. That will never happen.' Instead, she said, the focus should go on the next moment – work, breathing, or just a smile. 'You can do that for one minute,' she wrote. 'And if you can do one minute, you can do the next.'[11]

All of this is in line with the best-known talking treatment for conditions such as anxiety and depression – cognitive behavioural therapy, or CBT – which encourages people to try to break down situations that appear overwhelming. Therapists might work on whether there is a different way to perceive a particular event, or just an aspect of it. Or they might focus on a behaviour or action, and whether making even a small change would be beneficial.[12] The pioneers of these approaches, Albert Ellis and Aaron Beck, were both influenced by the Stoic school of philosophy, founded in Greece in around 300 BC.[13] Today, it is most often understood as steadfastness in the face of adversity, but that should not be confused with passivity. One of the main figures in Stoicism was Epictetus, who was born a slave and emphasised human beings' power to adjust their own perceptions and thus their feelings or emotions.[14]

Two thousand years later, rapid advances in technology have helped to increase researchers' interest in emotions, because they can now chart what happens in our brains when a particular set of feelings are experienced. Psychologist and broadcaster Claudia Hammond says that emotions used to be viewed as 'rather undefined concepts that had a deleterious influence on our behaviour by disrupting rational thinking'. Few were interested in studying them. 'They were considered difficult to measure and quantify; instead time was spent studying more rigorously defined topics like memory, perception and learning.'[15]

Now, understanding of all of these areas has benefited from advances in brain-scanning and neuroscience, with the central finding an immensely empowering one: our brains have the capacity to change throughout life, including in adulthood. One of the best-known examples of this 'neuroplasticity' was a study involving scans of the brains of London taxi drivers before and after they completed the gruelling 'Knowledge' test of the city's streets. As they went through the process of learning hundreds of routes, the grey matter in their hippocampus – the part of the brain associated with memory – was seen to enlarge.[16]

In his book *The Stress Test*, the clinical psychologist and neuroscientist Professor Ian Robertson explains how much this understanding of the brain as plastic transformed the prevailing orthodoxy that the adult brain was 'hard-wired'.

He believes that we can all learn to control our minds and emotions better, and then, within limits, turn stress to our advantage. The key is to try to control our perception of a particular situation, to see it as a challenge rather than a threat: 'A threat mindset focuses your mind on the possible downsides of the situation – making a fool of yourself, for example – while a challenge mindset turns your attention to the upsides – making your name, impressing others, or just doing a good job.' To push towards the challenge perception, he recommends telling yourself that any symptoms of anxiety, for example the heart beating faster or the stomach churning, are symptoms of excitement instead. Physical actions might help: deep breathing, squeezing pressure balls in your hand, or striking a confidence-boosting pose, however great the contrast with what you are actually feeling.[17]

I still have times I need to turn the fright into petrol – not on a straightforward news day but on the occasions when I am in the final stretch before a particularly big interview or up against difficult logistics. One morning just before Christmas 2014, I found myself at the school in Pakistan that had just been attacked in a heinous Taliban assault, killing more than 130 children. As I walked through its rooms, which had only just been cleared of the bodies, the gruesome evidence of what had happened was everywhere: discarded shoes and schoolbooks, bloodstains on the floor, the areas where the attackers had finally blown themselves up reduced to rubble. As I made my way to our makeshift live point on the crowded road outside, I felt deeply unsure as I took the microphone – battling to collect my thoughts and conscious of finding the right tone to convey the stark reality of what I had seen. There was little time to think, let alone to script and plan, as I would usually do. The only option was to focus on that next moment. And one at a time, the words came.

In Brief

Channel your nerves

When you feel that rush of anxiety, try to recognise it as a necessary part of gearing up for whatever it is that you are facing: the jolt or wake-up call that helps mark that next moment out as one to which you need to rise. See the frisson of nerves as something you can re-direct towards your goal and an energy that you can harness, rather than allow to take over.

Familiarity helps

Many of those we see performing brilliantly have been doing it for a long time, honing their skills over a sustained period. We might associate their success with raw talent, but it is far more likely that being exposed to a variety of experiences over time will have made an immense difference to their capacity to do their job. The lesson is therefore: don't stop too soon when you are engaged in a new and exacting task.

Break down the task before you

Having something especially daunting before you can feel overwhelming, but try to take it a step at a time. In my line of work that might simply be deciding how I want to begin an interview – what will my first question be? Figuring out the starting point should help the flow of thought onto the next question, and onwards from there.

Establish the routine that helps you perform

What you read first – how you practise, rehearse or revise – all of it can be part of a playbook that helps you rise to the occasion. Work out what suits you – rising early? Testing your recall in a particular way? Deploying that personal routine will help you focus on the practical and the useful, guarding against the mind dwelling too much on any nerves.

Owning It

Training is the answer to a great many things. You can do a lot if you are properly trained and I hope I have been

Queen Elizabeth II

Sometimes it is not just about getting through the next few minutes but about the big moments that have a particular importance in your life or to what you hope to do next – the job interview, appraisal, pay negotiation, business pitch, perhaps a media appearance. When I look through the glass that separates our studio from the green room outside in the mornings, I often remind myself how an environment so familiar to me will most likely be sparking apprehension among those waiting to come on the programme. What will they be asked? Will they have enough time to make their point, or will the time feel agonisingly long? Some will have done interviews before, and know that because of their work they will do so again, but for many, being on air will be a one-off event.

Whatever the level of preparation ahead of time, things can always go wrong on the day – even for those at the top of their game and with years of experience under their belt. In December 2016, the singer-songwriter Patti Smith had one of those agonising moments when a performance of hers went awry – and not just any performance, but the ceremony awarding that year's Nobel Prize in Literature to Bob Dylan. She had chosen one of her favourite Dylan songs to perform and spent every spare moment practising it, thinking about the message within each line. 'I sang the words to myself, over and over, in the original key, with pleasure and resolve. I had it in my mind to sing the song exactly as it was written and as well as I was capable of doing. I bought a new suit, I trimmed my hair, and felt that I was ready.'[1]

She took to the stage and began, accompanied by the Royal Stockholm Philharmonic Orchestra and watched by a live television audience. But two minutes into the song she stumbled over her words and came to a halt, the orchestra following suit. The cameras captured a mortified look on her face before she composed herself and did the best thing she could in the circumstances. 'I'm sorry,' she said, asking to pick up again, and perhaps most importantly, telling the audience: 'I'm so nervous.' They responded with a heartfelt round of applause and the song was duly completed. When she reflected later on what had happened, she said she had been overwhelmed by the moment: 'I was struck with a plethora of emotions, avalanching with such intensity that I was unable to negotiate them. I hadn't forgotten the words that were now a part of me. I was simply unable to draw them out.' At the Grammys in 2017, Adele had a similar experience when she asked to restart a tribute to the late George Michael. 'I can't mess this up for him,' she said, apologising and earning the support and respect of those watching.

My own high-stakes moments come in the form of big interviews, when it will be no use thinking later of the question that should have been asked, the fact that could have backed up an assertion, or the alternative view that would have been a useful response to a particular claim. There's never as much time to prepare as you would ideally like, and while some interviews are of the type that will come around again – a government minister, for example – others are unique. Prince Harry and Meghan Markle's engagement was the first time I had been asked to do a royal interview, and with more notice I would have taken a much more considered look back at what each of them had said in the past and at other royal engagement interviews. There was little time for any of that. Instead it was a question of working out how the conversation should feel, striking the balance between a happy moment for two people deciding to spend the rest of their lives together, and the fact that they were now both public figures.

Most pressingly, there would be a finite time to record, no chance to go over anything, and this was an opportunity that really would never come around again. I prepared the only way I know, by working out a structure – the topics I wanted to cover and a rough plan of the order in which they should come, starting with the story of the engagement but making sure I got to their families and their plans for the future. Without a structure I risked failing to ever get to some topics, but I also needed to be prepared to jump ahead or deviate from the plan, depending on what was said.

On that occasion I probably had about six topics I wanted to cover and twenty minutes in which to do it, but most of the time I think in terms of just three points – any more than that can become difficult to remember. It's an approach that can be applied to any significant conversation where you want to be setting or steering the agenda. Going into an interview, what are the three aspects of yourself you'd want remembered? In an appraisal, what are the three achievements you want to see acknowledged and recognised? In a pay negotiation, what is the evidence you will put forward in support of your case?

Whatever the setting, make sure your first point is not only a strong one but starts you off with the right tone. It needs to frame the conversation that will follow. If you're pitching for funding for a new business or idea – aim to sound convincing from the outset. To set a positive note at a work meeting – start with a recent success or acknowledge support received. However, if it has been called over a grievance or other difficulty – be prepared to address that straight away and back up your words with evidence. Keep it precise, neutral and professional – almost as if you are talking about someone else.

Plot your points on paper ahead of time and if there are obvious questions that will come up, such as in an annual evaluation of performance, make sure you have some answers. What went well over the last year? What's the aim for the next year? Note down every achievement or milestone in the relevant period and be ready to bring them up. Take confidence from the knowledge that you carry with you – you most likely know the detail of what you deal with every day better than the appraiser, and your mastery of it may be crucial to their ability to handle the level above. Have an answer to the probable question about weaknesses or 'areas of development', making it as positive as possible: perhaps by saying where you'd like to gain more experience or build on your understanding or skills.

It may feel awkward to be in the position of having to deliver a personal 'sell', but at times like this you have to find a way to do it. The alternative approach, being under-stated, effectively leaves the appraiser or interviewer with more to do in working out whether you are deserving of the outcome you seek. In her book, Professor Iris Bohnet says even self-evaluations can be a problem if some of those filling them in inflate their achievements, while others hold back. Citing studies identifying gender differences in self-confidence, she sounds the alarm over a practice common in many firms: employees asked to evaluate themselves, perhaps on a scale from one to ten, with the results then shared with supervisors.

She describes a scenario in which a manager might have two direct reports, a man and a woman, each of whom they would rate as a seven. 'But the male employee is overoptimistic about his abilities and the female employee under-confident; the former evaluates himself as a nine and the latter gives herself a five.' The manager knows both scores are a bit off but chooses to downgrade the man just a little – to an eight – while raising the woman to six. This is what's known as the anchoring effect, says Professor Bohnet. 'Inadvertently, subordinates have thrown a reference point at their managers who then cannot help but take it into account when making their own assessments.'[2]

Just as it can be easier to list someone else's strong points than identify your own, you may be well served by enlisting help ahead of an appraisal or evaluation-type process. Ask a colleague whose opinion you trust what they think your strengths are and how they think you should put yourself forward. As before, stick to a number easily remembered and work out how you would back up each assertion. Kamal Ahmed's view is that these should be facts not judgements, and as far as possible, uniquely applicable to you: 'Don't compare yourself to others, don't bring up something that might be a weakness in your experience and don't put doubt into the other person's mind.'

Malala Yousafzai, whose first big public moment came when she spoke at the United Nations on her sixteenth birthday and who later became the youngest ever Nobel laureate, also emphasises the importance of keeping it personal. She told me about a speech her father Ziauddin was once working on: 'In the first draft he prepared he included a series of quotes from important leaders. I tried to tell him that these people are already known to the world. People want to hear from *you*, so deliver your own message.' Now in demand as a speaker all over the world, she tries to keep her own statements and speeches focused. 'Be very well prepared in your mind on what you are going to talk about,' she told me. 'Never confuse yourself, always go with a very simple message of two or three key points. And keep it that way, so that people understand you. Don't use big, complicated words to show off.'

The work conversations or meetings most of us dread above all others are probably those to do with pay, especially if we instinctively feel that the act of asking for a raise will not be well received. There is evidence to suggest that that might well be true for women in particular. In 2005, a series of experiments led by Hannah Riley Bowles of Harvard's Kennedy School asked participants to evaluate CVs and interview notes on purported job candidates, as well as transcripts and video recordings of their interviews. The candidates were both male and female, and among the information given about each was whether they negotiated or attempted to negotiate on pay. The results suggested that male evaluators penalised women candidates attempting to negotiate for higher compensation. 'Men were significantly more inclined to work with nicer and less demanding women who accepted their compensation offers without comment,' concluded the authors. Interestingly, female evaluators were similarly punitive about the women, although in one experiment, where they had watched video recordings of the candidates, they appeared to be put off by both women and men who initiated pay negotiations and said they were not inclined to work with either.[3]

The nature of interviews and appraisals means that it's not easy to gather data from real-world rather than experimental settings, although researchers have drawn some conclusions from one particular workplace survey from Australia. Its data is useful, not only because it covers a wide range of employment but also because it includes specific questions on pay rises requested and obtained. A study of responses for the 2013–14 period found that while almost as many women as men reported asking for a pay rise, women were less successful in obtaining one. 'Women do ask but do not get,' said the authors. There was, however, a significant and encouraging picture within the responses from workers under the age of forty – in this group, there was no difference between the women's and men's success in getting a pay rise if they had asked for one.[4]

Women's worries about how they appear when negotiating on pay can even exist where the process is being handled by agents. After the 2014 Sony hack produced evidence of Hollywood's gender pay gap, revealing that the two female stars of *American Hustle* were on smaller deals than the three men, Jennifer Lawrence went public with an insight into what happened. She had received 7 per cent of the film's profits, as did Amy Adams, while Bradley Cooper, Christian Bale and Jeremy Renner all got 9 per cent. 'There was an element of wanting to be liked that influenced my decision to close the deal without a real fight,' she said. 'I didn't want to seem "difficult" or "spoiled". At the time, that seemed like a fine idea, until I saw the payroll on the internet and realised every man I was working with definitely didn't worry about being "difficult" or "spoiled". I don't think I'm the only woman with this issue. Are we socially conditioned to behave this way?'[5]

Lawrence acknowledged that her multi-million-dollar earnings meant that her problems 'aren't exactly relatable,' but reflected on how differently her male co-stars would likely be perceived. 'Jeremy Renner, Christian Bale, and Bradley Cooper all fought and succeeded in negotiating powerful deals for themselves. If anything, I'm sure they were commended for being fierce and tactical, while I was busy worrying about coming across as a brat.' For Natalie Portman, who was paid a third of the amount of her co-star Ashton Kutcher for the 2011 film *No Strings Attached*, the problem lay in the Hollywood system where a 'quote', or an individual's wage history, is used to determine pay for the next film. 'His was three times higher than mine so they said he should get three times more,' she said later, adding that she wasn't as angry at the time as she should have been. 'We get paid a lot, so it's hard to complain, but the disparity is crazy.'[6]

Linda Babcock and Sara Laschever, co-authors of the 2003 book *Women Don't Ask*, have urged women not to miss opportunities to negotiate on pay. One of their first studies looked at the starting salaries of men and women who had graduated from the MBA programme at Carnegie Mellon University. The men's salaries were 7.6 per cent, or nearly $4,000, higher than the women's. The vast majority of the women had accepted their employer's first salary offer, while most of the men had taken it as the opening of a negotiation. The women had lost out from what was probably no more than five minutes of discomfort, said

Babcock and Laschever. 'It's an unnecessary loss, because most employers expect people to negotiate and therefore offer less than they're prepared to pay.'[7]

Professor Heather McGregor's advice for anyone heading into a pay-related conversation is to do enough research in advance to produce a 'viable figure' for the job. She means a figure which is a realistic assessment of what the job is worth, including the circumstances of the employer. 'If you work in a small business with narrow margins, it just may not be possible to pay you the salary you deserve. In which case are the other benefits (flexibility and so on) worth the discount? If not, leave and get a role somewhere bigger.'[8]

Whatever the size of your employer, you might want to factor in whether there is job security that you might not get elsewhere, some particularly valuable experience to gain, or a location that suits your commute. If you ask for an increase and are told it's not possible, is there something else that could be – an enhanced title, development opportunity, perhaps working from home on a particular day of the week, thus saving on travel costs? If possible, secure a commitment for when the situation will be looked at again, and follow up with an email that covers not only what was agreed but records the requests you made, too.

While often high pressure, these big work moments can also be an opportunity to lay down a marker as to your future hopes and plans, or put forward something new. It might be an idea or project you'd like to pursue, or a suggestion that you think would make the office a better place. Or you might simply take the opportunity to ask the question of your appraiser or manager: what advice can they give you? In an interview situation too, you'd want to have a few questions up your sleeve and not necessarily all ones to do with the specific role you're going for. If you can raise broader points too – about the business climate or the level of competition in the industry – it all serves as evidence of a thoughtful, enquiring mind. And it may just be what makes you the person they remember.

In Brief

Distil your message

Most of us will go into big moments or meetings with too much to say, which carries the risk that your speech comes out as a long train of thought rather than a considered set of messages. To avoid this, work out in advance the points you want to get across – ideally not more than three. Think of these as your headlines. You may expand on one more than the other, but make sure that whatever you are asked, you deliver those three points. You need to make it as easy as possible for the other party to remember clearly what was important to you and why as they leave.

Keep it rooted in fact

Beware of basing your message on how you feel you should be treated or what you deserve. Instead, be concrete about what you *have* achieved and delivered and what you want to do next. Think about specific requests and place them in a range – some may be easier to deliver than others, perhaps a training course or development opportunity. Do your research in advance so that you keep the conversation grounded in fact, which is especially important if it is a pay discussion. Arm yourself with knowledge gleaned in advance – if you are trusted and respected by colleagues, there is much more chance they will be open with you about their circumstances.

Start with the right tone

Think about which of your points you want to open with and the tone you want to strike. As the customer service adage goes: they may not remember what you said but they will remember how you made them feel. Is your tone going to be open and enthusiastic or serious and concerned? Are you going to start with the trickiest of your points or build up to it? All of this can affect your chances of getting your desired outcome.

Rising Up

The free bird leaps on the back of the wind
… and dares to claim the sky

Maya Angelou

It takes one set of skills to rise to the challenge of a particularly intense moment, but quite another to have staying power in a position at or close to the top of your chosen arena. From the sprint-like process of delivering what you need to under pressure, reaching and holding on to a senior role is a longer game.

In my field, these are the roles that put you in the privileged position of being able to question others – particularly the powerful – in the most public way, and you need to be perceived as having the right to be there. The first time I thought about the process that gets you to that point was about a decade ago, when I was wondering if I had the capability to one day present a high-profile news programme. I asked a senior BBC executive what she thought it took. 'You need authority,' she told me.

It made absolute sense, and yet I had little idea how to develop this quality. Did it depend on being particularly talented from the outset? Being around the block for a sufficient length of time, earning your stripes? Or was it more down to good fortune and a series of opportunities coming your way?

It didn't help that there were precious few examples that came to mind of women in the most authoritative broadcasting roles. At times of national or historical importance – elections, state occasions or royal events – it is men who have tended to lead the coverage and guide audiences through what is happening. They're often referred to as 'distinguished' or having 'gravitas' – again words that are rarely used to describe women – and visible signs of ageing, such as grey hair, burnish the image.

Today, prime political slots on television on both sides of the Atlantic are dominated by male hosts, the Sunday morning shows being the most obvious example. In the UK it took until 2017 for a woman – Sophy Ridge of Sky – to have her own show in one of those prestigious slots. In 2015, *Vanity Fair* celebrated the 'titans of late night television' in the US with a photograph of ten hosts – all male.

Ten years on from my own musings on how to develop authority, I have an answer to the question I found so perplexing. The route to authority is knowledge – and a willingness to demonstrate it in a sustained fashion. For me, that means being as well informed as possible and then using that knowledge, whether on air or behind the

scenes – for others it may be the work meeting that provides the most regular opportunity to demonstrate what you know. It's always worth going into these with a prepared comment, idea or question – something to throw into the mix and establish the credentials of being a participant rather than a silent onlooker. It may fall by the wayside as the conversation moves in a different direction, but going in armed with something to say puts you into a state of readiness.

You might choose to root your contribution in what someone else present has said, portraying it as a follow-up, or you might nudge those present towards a new direction or consideration of an otherwise overlooked area. If your own point is then validated by others, all the better. During

Barack Obama's first term in the White House, when two-thirds of his top aides were men, the *Washington Post* reported how female staffers launched a concerted effort to get their voices heard. 'When a woman made a key point, other women would repeat it, giving credit to its author,' wrote correspondent Juliet Eilperin. 'This forced the men in the room to recognise the contribution.' The result they observed was that the president noticed, and began calling more often on women and junior aides in the meetings.[1]

Having women in high-profile positions gives them prominence and power, and that basic construct is one that the classicist Mary Beard believes we should see in the context of the weight of thousands of years of history. The striking and memorable female characters in Greek myth and storytelling, she explains, are not figures to emulate. 'They are portrayed as abusers rather than users of power. They take it illegitimately, in a way that leads to chaos, to the fracture of the state, to death and destruction. In fact, it is the unquestionable mess that women make of power in Greek myth that justifies their exclusion from it in real life and justifies the rule of men.'[2]

In the modern age, some female leaders would probably argue they had faced a disproportionate focus on their personal relationships and the actions of those close to them. In Pakistan, Benazir Bhutto was dogged by corruption allegations against her husband, nicknamed 'Mr 10 Percent'; while in South Korea, Park Geun-hye's downfall came after a row over the alleged undue influence of a longtime female friend accused of corruption.

It's not that women politicians haven't made mistakes or errors of judgement, but consider the nature of the insults that can be hurled at them. As the first female prime minister of Australia, Julia Gillard's experience included being portrayed naked in cartoons and a menu at an opposition fundraising event including a dish described as 'Julia Gillard Quail – Small Breasts, Huge Thighs and a Big Red Box'.[3] At demonstrations, placards against her policies called her a bitch and the opposition leader, Tony Abbott, was even photographed in front of one emblazoned with the words 'Ditch the Witch'.

No wonder she then rounded on him in a parliamentary speech, telling him that if he wanted to know 'what misogyny looks like in modern Australia, he doesn't need a motion in the House of Representatives, he needs a mirror'. The video of the speech went viral, but less than a year later, Abbott was Australia's prime minister.[4] When she looked back, Julia Gillard concluded that something deep-seated was at play: 'Somewhere in our brains is whispering a stereotype that says if a woman is leading, commanding, she has probably given up on "female" traits of empathy, likeability; she's probably a bit hard-boiled.'[5]

The psychologist Professor Susan Fiske's work on stereotyping has looked at categories of people and the perception of two qualities in particular: warmth and competence. She says her findings suggest that there is a trade-off for women when they move away from traditional roles. They are then less likely to be perceived as warm, which she describes as a catch-22 situation that competent men will not experience.[6] In one study she led with Amy Cuddy, where participants were asked to rate certain groups on the basis of how they were viewed by American society as a whole, there was a marked contrast between the perception of housewives – high warmth, low competence – and businesswomen – high competence but moderate warmth.[7]

Any warmth-competence trade-off presents the woman politician with a particular dilemma because they need to demonstrate both qualities – the competence that makes them suitable for high office and the warmth to appeal to voters. At least, that's how it seems now. Women of an earlier time, such as Margaret Thatcher and Indira Gandhi, seem to have been largely unencumbered by questions about likeability. Gandhi's early battle was against low expectations – when veteran leaders in her party first put her forward as a candidate for office they called her a 'dumb doll', thinking she was useful for her family name and as the daughter of a prime minister, but could be easily controlled.

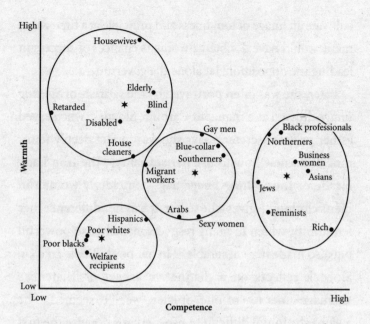

Her manner was, in many ways, as her biographer Sagarika Ghose has noted, 'more man than woman', which Ghose attributes to her personal and family circumstances. 'She was a very rare only child in the early twentieth century and also a girl child. And as the eldest child of the eldest son, who in that traditional situation would've been expected to be male, she had to live up to certain masculine ideas of power.'[8]

For Thatcher, the 'Iron Lady' label first bestowed upon her by a Russian journalist in 1976, when she was a relatively new Conservative Party leader, proved useful not only in the Cold War context but at home, too.[9] It helped cultivate an image of toughness and principle at a time when many would have doubted a woman's chances of success in leading the opposition, let alone the government.

Later, she was often portrayed by the satirists of *Spitting Image* dressed as a man, but Caroline Slocock, who served as her private secretary, says she was in fact deeply feminine and knew how to use her sexuality: 'The Iron Lady facade or the *Spitting Image* hag – an elderly woman in men's clothing – gives a lie to her. It was her difference, her femininity, which in many respects made her so powerful but also made her vulnerable.'[10] In her book *People Like Us*, Slocock reflects on a distinctive aspect of Thatcher's language – her use of 'one', or later, 'we': '"I" seemed to be a word she found difficult to use, perhaps because the first person for a woman lacked sufficient authority at that time, perhaps because she wanted to hide behind a more impersonal, or even collective, identity. Women should not be seen to be pushy and being self-effacing was (and still is) seen as attractive.'

Fast-forward to Hillary Clinton's two presidential runs and the questions that pursued her both times about whether she was likeable. In January 2008, she was asked directly what she would say to voters who were hesitating 'on the likeability issue'. She dealt with it with spirit, and the riposte from her Democratic rival Barack Obama, 'You're likeable enough, Hillary' was widely disparaged.

But the point stuck, and surfaced again when she was up against Donald Trump in 2016.

Later, Clinton said she thought there was a key shift in people's opinion of her once she was running for the White House. 'When I was Secretary of State, I came out of it with a 69 per cent approval rating, because I was in service to my country. I was in service to our President. But, when a woman walks into the arena and says, "I'm doing this for myself," it really does have a dramatic effect on how people perceive.'[11] The same could be said, however, of a man who had been in a similar position in government and was then putting himself forward for the top job – different standards apply as people weigh up whether someone is a worthy contender for the most pre-eminent role.

In business, the jump from second-in-command to the top is a particularly big one to make and some women who have done it – or almost done it – have felt they ran into barriers they weren't prepared for. When Susan Chira asked the question 'Why don't more women get that No 1 job?' for a *New York Times* report in 2017, a pattern of experience emerged from the executives and former executives she spoke to: 'Women are often seen as dependable, less often as visionary. Women tend to be less comfortable with self-promotion – and more likely to be criticized when they do grab the spotlight. Men remain threatened by assertive women. Most women are not socialized to be unapologetically competitive. Some women get discouraged and drop out along the way. And many are disproportionately penalized for stumbles.'[12] She concluded that 'women who aspire to power evoke far more resistance, both overt and subtle, than they expected would be the case by now.'

I find myself increasingly aware that with women in senior or powerful positions, we often want to know what they are like as a person, to go alongside our judgement about their professional or leadership capability. Are they friendly? Easy to get along with? Or are they the opposite – forceful, aggressive, even a 'ball-breaker'?

The sociologist Marianne Cooper says that even at moments of particular success for individual women, the focus can swiftly turn to their personal characteristics. She cites the case of Jill Abramson, the first woman executive editor of the *New York Times*, who in 2013 had just celebrated her newspaper winning four Pulitzer Prizes when she became the subject of an article in which anonymous staff described her as stubborn, condescending and unreasonable.[13] 'If a woman acts assertively or competitively, if she pushes her team to perform, if she exhibits decisive and forceful leadership,' she says, 'she is deviating from the social script that dictates how she "should" behave.'[14]

Theresa May told me one of the problems she sees with women's progression to the top of the business world is that employers are less likely to be willing to take a chance on them: 'For a woman to be able to show her authority and ability, it is often about demonstrating that a job *has* been done, rather than being identified as someone with potential.' When key appointments are being made, she said, the search is usually for people with a particular set of experience. 'The women often have experience in a different part of the company – they might be more likely to be on the HR side, corporate relations or marketing, not on the finance side. There are exceptions to this, of course, but when nomination companies look for experience they look at what you've done. And if women haven't done it, they don't ask "Are they capable of doing it?"'

Where companies *do* turn to senior women, there is evidence that it is often at times of particular difficulty – which in turn carries a greater risk for those coming in and tasked with sorting things out. Professors Michelle Ryan and Alex Haslam of Exeter University have called this the 'glass cliff', after looking into individual companies' circumstances at the time they made female and male appointments to their boards. It revealed that firms appointing women to board positions were more likely to have experienced consistently poor performance in the previous few months than those appointing men. 'In this way, such women can be seen to be placed on top of a "glass cliff", in the sense that their leadership appointments are made in problematic organisational circumstances and hence are more precarious,' they wrote. There was a greater risk of failure, they said, for which the women may be singled out for blame, while the situation they had to deal with was largely forgotten.[15]

Christine Lagarde, who herself took over at the International Monetary Fund after it had been rocked by a sex scandal involving its previous director, also thinks that women are 'generally given space and appointed to jobs when the situation is tough. In times of crisis, women eventually are called upon to sort out the mess, face the difficult issues and be completely focused on restoring the situation.'[16]

It's not something Theresa May agreed with when I spoke to her in 10 Downing Street while she was still in the honeymoon period of her brief time in power. 'The Conservative Party is the one party in this country that's had two women in this building,' she told me. 'I don't think they saw it as putting a woman in because of a particular issue to be dealt with.' Perhaps she was already conscious of the risks of being seen as a rescue or saviour figure – even if you do resolve the situation you inherit, you may then have outlived your usefulness.

What does seem to be happening more now than in the past is the appointment of women to senior and authoritative roles later in life. Janet Yellen was sixty-seven when she was appointed to lead the US Federal Reserve and Mary Beard's television career didn't begin until she was in her mid-fifties. Margaret Hodge, who was fifty when first elected an MP and became the chair of a powerful parliamentary committee at sixty-five, thinks her experience demonstrates the possibilities of a woman taking a longer-term perspective. 'The time when we tend to have our children coincides with the point when society tells us we should be climbing towards the top of the career ladder. What should be the very best years of our lives rapidly become the hardest as we struggle to marry two important ambitions and feel guilt about not fulfilling either role properly,' she says. 'Yet if life is a marathon, why can't you coast in your paid job for a few years, while your children are young, and return to the competitive fray when they become more independent? Those few years out of the race do not diminish your ability to contribute or succeed later, when you are a little older.'[17]

One woman who has had not only a second but a third act in her own career is Chile's first female president, Michelle Bachelet. She suffered considerable trauma in the early part of her life, when the military coup that brought Augusto Pinochet to power in 1973 saw her father arrested and tortured, later dying in custody, while she and her mother were taken to a secret prison. After qualifying as a doctor and later becoming active in politics, she used to reflect upon how incongruous her rise might appear in a deeply Catholic country: 'I am a woman, a socialist, divorced and agnostic, all the sins together.' But in the end she served two terms as president and also became the founder director of the UN Women organisation. All along, she has understood the power of the symbol and the role model: 'As a doctor, when I was minister of health and would go somewhere, little girls would come up to me and say, "I want to be like you one day, I want to be a doctor." Now, they tell me, "I want to be President just like you." All of us can dream as big as we want.'[18]

In Brief

Developing authority

This is an essential attribute as you rise in seniority, but it can be hard to know how you can nurture it – as well as how to demonstrate it to others. I think of it as two parts – the acquisition of knowledge and the willingness to deploy and share that knowledge. You need to know your stuff – whatever your field – and then be prepared to show what you know, rather than hold back.

Making sure you are heard

Many of the settings in which you need to demonstrate authority can be daunting – such as meetings where you are the outsider, or the most junior in the room. Go in with one prepared thought or question and tell yourself your voice *will* be heard in that particular gathering. It may be that you end up contributing something different to what you envisaged, but having something up your sleeve before you walk into the room will build your confidence.

Be authentic, be consistent

Rising in seniority and responsibility in your role means your judgements will start to affect a greater range of people and outcomes. Establish a leadership style that suits your strengths and interests. Are you the problem solver? The detail or the big picture person? The one to turn to in a crisis? The one who will help persuade other members of the team? People need to know when to turn to you, what they can expect from you and be able to trust you to deliver.

Play the long game

Don't scale back your ambitions if you have taken time out or had an unusual career path. We have many more examples today of older women's experience and insight being valued as they return to the workplace or go for a career change. Don't lose heart, or hope!

Resilience

Remember to look up at the stars
and not down at your feet

Professor Stephen Hawking

A few days before the UK general election in June 2017, I opened the *Daily Mail* on my way to work early one morning to see my own face splashed across one of the inside pages. It was an article sparked by a combative interview with Boris Johnson the previous day. I had had a miserable week, it said, first appearing out of my depth when moderating – or 'failing to moderate' – a televised leaders' debate and then deploying an 'aggressive, even menacing tone' in that 'car crash' interview. A complaint had gone straight to the BBC within minutes of that interview ending, I read, and after a previously glittering record, it said I could now be called the BBC's former Golden Girl.

It was a crushing way to start the day. By then I had thought that I was accustomed to the scrutiny that came with the job, but the barbs in the article – especially those that it said had come from anonymous colleagues – hit me hard.[1] I should, however, have been better prepared, because that sort of coverage would have come sooner or later and is also bound to happen again. The nature of my work, particularly as a journalist employed by a public broadcaster, makes it inevitable. That didn't, however, make it any easier to read such a withering take on my abilities. What did make a difference was something very simple: the passage of time. From being able to think of little else first thing in the morning the piece seemed much less important that evening and by the following day, it had further receded from my mind.

Perhaps that process will be quicker the next time round, but my aim is for a balance between being alive to feedback and criticism – because I don't ever want to stop learning – and not letting myself be derailed by it. Natalie Portman has described how it feels for actors, whose work requires great sensitivity and empathy but who will invariably face bad reviews as well as good ones: 'You have to be very emotionally ready, emotionally connected to everything, but then, as a public figure, you have to have such a thick skin. People will say such harsh things. You need to be vulnerable for your work, but you also need to be tough as nails just to keep up, and that combination is really hard to maintain.'[2] Hillary Clinton's approach is to listen, but try not to take it personally: 'You should take criticism seriously because you might learn something, but you can't let it crush you. You have to be resilient to keep moving forward whatever the personal setbacks and even insults that come your way.'[3]

At different stages of life, and to different degrees, all of us will face outcomes we would rather have avoided, and most of us will struggle with how to pick ourselves up and carry on. We will all have a different definition of what constitutes a hard knock, or a disappointment, or a set of results that will alter our future paths, and these can affect our belief in ourselves. But that does not always happen – some of us dwell on adverse eventualities more than others. This is what the clinical psychologist Norman Garmezy, regarded as a pioneer of our understanding of resilience, sought to understand when he started to visit schools across the United States, asking them about children with the most challenging circumstances at home who were nevertheless managing to thrive and become a source of pride to their teachers. What made that possible?[4]

His work opened the way to theories about individual responses to adversity and difficulty, and how much they might depend on the characteristics of a particular child or external factors from which they benefited. In the 1980s, an extraordinary three-decade study of children in Hawaii was published by psychologists Emmy Werner and Ruth Smith, after they had tracked an entire cohort of children born on one of the islands in the year 1955. Of those from families with a range of difficulties and stress, including poverty and mental illness, about a third grew into competent, confident and caring adults.[5] By the age of forty, not one of this group was unemployed, relying on social services or in trouble with the law. 'Their very existence,' wrote Professor Werner, 'challenges the myth that a child who is a member of a so-called "high-risk" group is fated to become one of life's losers.'

She identified a set of 'protective factors' that could be seen in these children – including their own personalities and talents, bonds with at least one emotionally stable person in the family, or support in the community – while also noting that there were others, outside this group, who had had problems but then staged a recovery by the time they reached mid-life. These 'troubled teens' who then went on to achieve stability later in life were more likely to be female, with educational opportunities, good relationships and marriages playing a role. Overall, there was a discernible gender aspect to her results in Hawaii: 'We have consistently noted that a higher proportion of females than males managed to cope effectively with adversity in childhood and adulthood. They relied more frequently on informal sources of social support than the men.'

For her book *Rising Strong*, Brené Brown looked at a range of people who had experienced and overcome failure, identifying that what they shared was a deep understanding of their emotions and a high tolerance for discomfort. In other words, their resilience was not because they had such a thick skin that they brushed off or ignored what had happened to them, but because they took stock of it. How they perceived a particular event or situation was crucial. 'When something difficult happens,' she says, 'our brain scrambles to make up a story about what happened. And often those stories are not true.'[6] She gives an example from her own life, when she perceived a statement from her husband that there was nothing in their fridge to make a sandwich with to be a criticism of her – she had 'failed' to do the shopping.

What she believes resilient men and women have in common is that they are good at being uncomfortable. 'They say, "This project failed at work. What can I learn from this? What is true about what happened? What is not true about what happened? What role did I play? What can I do differently next time?"' And she says they remain in this state of discomfort and uncertainty 'long enough to figure out what is really going on'. It may be that the time required to get to a more measured conclusion about what happened is short – perhaps just a few minutes. But employing a process like this is a way of allowing you to be open to feedback and absorb any valid points without losing your nerve for the future.

Yet sometimes it is really not worth engaging with what is thrown in your direction. When I talked to Malala Yousafzai for this book, I asked her about coping with criticism, because however much she is lauded around the world, she has at times faced hostility in her home country of Pakistan. There are those who resent her high profile, saying that there are 'many Malalas', many other girls who have overcome hurdles in order to go to school – although that ignores the fact that when she spoke out on television against the Taliban at the tender age of eleven, few adult women or men were prepared to do the same. Other accusations are more sinister, calling her an agent of Western countries.

Malala told me she tries to keep the criticism at a distance. 'I think it's very healthy to keep yourself away from negative thoughts and comments, but it is reality that they will come your way. If it is fair criticism that does make sense and is justified with reasons, then look at it and check if you are on the right track.' But she is also determined not to allow any negativity to hold her back. 'There are people who won't accept you even if you are an angel. If you get lost in thinking about that, you will lose focus on your key goal and your key aims. My aim is to work for girls' education and I don't want to be distracted from that.'

But what if, however hard you try and however much you *know* you need to forget about the presentation that bombed, the harsh verdict on a performance, or the job you didn't get, you cannot dislodge it from your mind? You might feel that it's hanging over you, that everyone you come across is thinking about it as they see you. In Katty Kay and Claire Shipman's book *The Confidence Code*, they have a suggestion shared by neuroscientist Laura-Ann Pettito, who had a particular personal doubt about her public speaking ability.

Every time she gave a speech, she would ruminate afterwards on how she might have done better. And then she decided that, instead, she'd spend time reminding herself of three things she had done well. 'Now when the negative ruminations start, she consciously goes through her list of achievements and successes: "That was a good paper I finished," the interior monologue might now go. "I got that lab report done quicker than I expected. I had a good conversation with my new grad student."'[7]

Note how these statements are very real, based on actual encounters and actions in the individual's life. They are not big, abstract assertions along the lines of 'I am better than this', or 'I know I can nail it next time' – although these may help some people feel better. Katty Kay says we should reflect on what is now known from the science on neuroplasticity. 'With repetition, you can train the brain not to ruminate. And you need to realise – you're not everyone else's headline. We might think everyone's talking about our failures but generally people are too busy with their own lives to spend time on yours. After all, how much time do you spend on other people's professional problems? Not much.'

When the psychologist Professor Joanne Wood led a study on the effect of positive self-statements on how people feel about themselves, she and her co-authors found that in some cases, they could backfire. In one experiment, participants were cued at different points to repeat to themselves the words 'I'm a lovable person'. A subsequent analysis of mood and self-esteem led the authors to conclude that the only people to experience a boost from repeating the statement were those who went into the experiment with already high self-esteem. 'When people with low self-esteem repeated the statement, neither their feelings about themselves nor their moods improved – they got worse.' The researchers could not be sure why this was, but suggested that outlandish, unreasonably positive self-statements might spark contradictory thoughts, similar to the effect of overblown praise.[8]

The moments that require you to summon resilience will by definition be hard, even painful, but these are also likely to be the times when you learn the most, including about your own character and capabilities. In a letter the poet Ted Hughes wrote to his son Nicholas, he said that the moments in which life takes us by surprise and where we are thrown into the front line are also where we come alive and have to call up our innermost resources. 'The only calibration that counts is how much heart people invest, how much they ignore their fears of being hurt or caught out or humiliated,' he wrote. 'And the only thing people regret is that they didn't live boldly enough, that they didn't invest enough heart, didn't love enough. And that's how we measure out our real respect for people – by the degree of feeling they can register, the voltage of life they can carry and tolerate – and enjoy.'[9]

These are the moments that will test our capabilities, but we need to find a way through them and out the other side. Most of us will be able to point to setbacks in our own lives that were crushing at the time but much less so when we look back on them – we went to a university other than our first choice, we ended up at a different employer and it turned out fine or better, our broken hearts were mended. What we need to work out is the thought process that is not about shaking off every criticism – or conversely regarding every negative experience as a disaster – but one that puts it into a manageable place and context. It might not sweep away the disappointment, the bad review, the scathing feedback from your boss or the niggling undermining of your achievements, but it will help you move on from it. Most likely, it will leave you stronger and more capable of facing the next test that comes along.

In Brief

Dealing with criticism

It's never going to be pleasant to get this sort of feedback, but work out a way of dealing with it. You need to establish if there are valid points that you need to take on board and learn from. See it as being in your own interests to do so, to avoid making the same mistake again. If the comments come from someone whose judgement you rate and trust, but who hasn't been able to articulate an alternative approach, try to get them to be more specific. Not just that this didn't work, but what might have been a better route for you to take – or what would they suggest you do in future?

Don't lose your nerve

Failures and setbacks are unsettling and dispiriting and there is no getting away from that. But once you have learned what you need to, focus on moving on. Think in terms of turning to a new page rather than continuing to dwell on the previous one. Don't allow yourself to be derailed – you need to be able to hold your nerve the next time you face something similar.

resilience

It goes with the territory

I know that I cannot have the privileges of my job without the scrutiny that comes alongside, and that helps to give me some perspective when things go wrong. Some people will never like you or your work, for reasons beyond your control – and even a small amount of public exposure can attract vitriol from strangers. Learn to differentiate between that negativity and that which is worth your time.

Balance

———————

Love is the only thing that we can
carry with us when we go

Louisa May Alcott

A work–life balance is so elusive for most of us that it took me a long time to feel that I had anything useful to contribute on the subject. The term implies that a point can be reached where these two aspects of our lives are in sync, but of course the truth is that few of us will feel we ever get there – and if we do it is more than likely to be temporary. Sometimes, opportunities arise but we're not in a position to take them up, at other times work is going well but there is much else that you might wish for that is missing.

My experience has been easier than that of many other working parents, for three reasons. I married a decent human being who pulls his weight at home, my children have been blessed with good health, and from the time they were born I have had a job that enabled me to afford the childcare I needed to continue working as I had before – including accommodating weekends, anti-social hours and international travel.

But with three children twenty months apart there was still plenty to grapple with: three lots of nappies, a washing machine running 24/7, and mealtimes that a visiting friend said reminded her of feeding time at the zoo. I was filming a documentary in India when all three boys and their father came down with chicken pox, mournfully displayed to me via FaceTime, and there was hassle that I unnecessarily brought upon myself: following up on a delivery of blinds when I was several time zones away, and doing the online supermarket shop from Beijing because I realised the house was perilously close to running out of nappies.

In that period, and since, I've always been keen to know how other working parents do things. How do they manage their childcare, what happens in the school holidays, who does the cooking? To this day, a part of me is in search of the magical, probably tech-based solution that makes everything easier at home – some sort of wonder app that generates a weekly menu and shopping list perfect for your family's tastes and deals with diaries, commitments and domestic admin.

Short of such a life hack, the single most useful thing I have learned goes back to that sense of a life in phases: there will be periods when your hands may be full in the most literal sense, with little creatures requiring feeding, changing and bathing. At other times you may finally be able to reintroduce weekend lie-ins but the dramas are more grown-up and complex, and in yet another set of circumstances the needs of elderly or sick family members mean that priorities have to change. Of course, life doesn't come at you in neatly packaged sections, with the end of one phase and the beginning of another clearly marked. The most difficult times will be when the intense challenges come all at once, especially when they relate to situations that cannot be changed, however hard you try, like ill health or the breakdown of a relationship.

The sociologist Professor Phyllis Moen thinks that rather than speaking of 'work and life' or 'work and family', we should use the term 'life course fit' as a way to describe the demands on us coming from different quarters, at different stages. 'The diversity of the workforce in terms of age, family responsibilities, and household composition is simply not captured under the "work-family" rubric,' she says, and it may also mask where the real problems lie. 'I have come to the conclusion, after thirty years of research, that it is really the conditions of work that promote the greatest stress and overload,' she says.

She points to how much has changed in terms of family life in that period – women working as well as men, couples having fewer or no children and having them later in life, and the rise of single households. 'What hasn't changed are the toxic working conditions based on the career mystique of continuous full-time, exclusive dedication to work, a mystique based on the breadwinner/ homemaker model.' While that model is largely obsolete, she points out that the structure of the workplace is still built around it: 'As long as we're talking about "work-family," we're privileging the idea that the problem arises from the intersection of those two. And yet, single workers also experience stress as a result of overload, time pressures, and the idea of being available 24/7. All of this has nothing to do with the family side.'[1] What we need instead, Moen believes, are flexible career templates that could accommodate a broader range of options for male and female workers of all ages. This might mean looking afresh at what constitutes working hours, a working week or a career path. In this way, she says, there could be a renovated concept of 'flexible careers': a 'fruitful way of framing and contextualizing the dynamics of "work" and "family" as they are played out in individual lives, in families, in communities, and in contemporary society.'[2]

What I have learned from many conversations with my own colleagues in the last year – sparked by the BBC pay row but leading to a much broader debate about women and work – is that what we have at present doesn't, in truth, offer much flexibility or choice. My industry, broadcast news, is a twenty-four-hour, shift-based operation, where some women become part-time because it is the only way they can have certainty about working hours and be able to set up childcare accordingly. If they later want to return to full-time, perhaps when children reach school age, the option may no longer be there, or they may find their part-time experience is under-valued. Or they may have been freelance, as many people who work in broadcasting and content production, particularly outside of news, are. This poses another problem: how can you set up childcare when you don't know how much work you will have and when projects typically last for just a few months?

Phyllis Moen had the opportunity to see a version of her ideas in action through a real-world study involving the consumer electronics company Best Buy, which had decided to roll out a programme for some employees called ROWE – Results Only Work Environment. She and her collaborator Erin Kelly monitored the impact of the initiative, which is based on the employees carrying out their work when and where it suits them. All that matters is the results achieved.

The hardest part was being clear at the outset in identifying what those results should be, because so much of our understanding of work revolves around turning up at a certain location and interacting face-to-face with peers and managers. 'All of us are socialized to take as "given" the clocks and calendars guiding our lives,' says Professor Moen. 'We assume Monday is the first day of the work week, that eight (or more) hours, five (or more) days a week is what work is. Simply being at work equals productivity and dedication.' Being part of ROWE turned this idea on its head for the employees involved, but at the end of six months they were more satisfied and the turnover of staff members was lower. The teams also communicated better, because they had had to – work was being handed over from one to the other without them meeting. They had been able to avoid the rush-hour commute, take parents to doctor's appointments, get to school meetings and schedule their work accordingly.[3]

A system like that won't be applicable to every team in every company or organisation, but bringing it in where possible would make for happier and more productive employees. It would also reduce some of the tortuous ways by which people end up having to be shifty about their caring responsibilities lest these make them 'look bad' at work. I know two lawyers – one barrister and one solicitor – who were told by senior figures never to say that children were the reason they needed to leave work at a particular time. A foreign correspondent based in London wonders, when she rings her newsdesk back home and they ask how her children are, whether it means their primary perception of her is as a woman with responsibilities that reduce her commitment to them. And I too find myself hesitating when my colleagues ask me to do a pre-record for the next morning's programme and I know the post-school time slot will make it difficult. Do I mention I'll be busy with children at that time, or just say I am unavailable?

Thinking in terms of phases or life course fit means that bigger decisions, such as a possible move to a new job or new role, might be weighed up simply on the basis of what feels right at the present time, while keeping an open mind about longer-term horizons. When Jo Swinson was re-elected as a Liberal Democrat MP in 2017, it was just as there was a vacancy for the post of party leader. She was immediately spoken of as a credible candidate with a good chance of success, and one who would break new ground in a party that has not had enough women in Parliament. At the time she had a three-year-old son, but when she announced her decision not to stand, she was careful to speak in broad terms rather than close off future possibilities: 'Being the leader of a political party is a unique and all-encompassing job, even more than the roles of MP and Minister that I have undertaken before. It should not be done simply to achieve status, to make a point, or to please others.'[4] Two years later, her choice was a different one: having had a second child, she stood for party leader and won.

Women of an earlier generation made their own choices, albeit with much less of a roadmap available and precious few role models. 'Work–life balance was a term not yet coined in the years my children were young,' wrote Ruth Bader Ginsburg in 2016, by which time she had served on the US Supreme Court for more than two decades.[5] She credited her father-in-law for the advice that helped her in the 1950s, when she was deeply apprehensive about studying the law with a one-year-old child. 'Ruth, if you don't want to start law school, you have a good reason to resist the undertaking,' he told her. 'No one will think the less of you if you make that choice. But if you really want to study law, you will stop worrying and find a way to manage child and school.' The future judge's way was to go off to her classes at 8.30 a.m. and return home to 'children's hour' with her daughter at 4 p.m. 'After Jane's bedtime, I returned to the law books with renewed will. Each part of my life provided respite from the other and gave me a sense of proportion that classmates trained only on law studies lacked.'

Thinking through the capacity you have at any given point in time really does matter. I love what I do now but I don't think *Today* would have been the right place for me either earlier in my career, when I had less experience, or when my children were still waking up in the night. At different points, I've tried to find solutions that worked for our family and put them into place not for ever, but for as long as they made sense. And I needed to have some sort of framework to help me evaluate everyday commitments, a way of sifting through what I could say yes to and what I should decline. When my children were younger, it was relatively easy to put them to bed at 7 p.m. and know that, unless they were ill, I could work undisturbed or book a babysitter without them even knowing I had been out of the house. Now it's more complicated – the evenings are longer, there's homework to think about and needs are more complex. And so I am much less likely to take on an evening commitment to chair a panel or attend a screening, however interesting it may sound – at least for now.

The mental checklist or filter helps me to find a way through a landscape that is not only about the nuclear family and the job. What makes us rounded human beings, alive to the world around us, is about so much more – community, charity and decency. Women's lives tend to be full of seemingly small but time-consuming tasks – the organisation of the home and perhaps the office too, the marshalling of resources, the remembering of milestones and special occasions. But beyond that, when I am weighing up what should be a yes and what I can't manage – however much I might like to – I think about who or what is at the heart of the request. My mother's singing group asking me to speak at their concert is a no-brainer, as is the small charity set up by a friend that has few other avenues of potential support. But I always try to focus on where I can add value – I have no qualifications to be a trustee but maybe I can help out by hosting an event or doing something else that is a better fit with my skills.

Once you establish your checklist, it needs to apply whether the commitment is next month or in a year's time – it's all too easy to put something in the diary in advance without thinking through how it will feel when it's coming up tomorrow. I also know my limitations; while some of my colleagues can go out the night before an early shift, I need my sleep. I try to space out what does go into the diary, guarding against commitments piling up too close to each other, but there are still times I look at it and my heart sinks. My hope is to keep the intense periods as the exception rather than the norm, but if I do find myself hurtling about and getting ground down in the process, I remind myself of one of my grandmother's favourite Urdu sayings: *'harkat may barkat'* – there are blessings in being busy.

I also know I'm fortunate to have a significant degree of choice in how my schedule operates beyond my core working hours, unlike those whose days in the office can stretch into the evening with events that are difficult to dodge, especially if they involve clients. When Carolyn Fairbairn was appointed to lead the Confederation of British Industry, she wasted no time in taking issue with the business dinner, a concept that she felt excluded far too many people. 'A lot of women – and I was one of them because I was bringing up three kids – just want to go home,' she said. 'Why not have more early evening events like a panel discussion, a nice glass of wine or two and then everyone off home by 7.30? Maybe the business dinner is a vestige of old business life.'[6]

It's not only mothers, of course, but fathers too – and indeed anyone in search of a decent balance in their lives – who would welcome the working day being kept to sensible parameters. The problem is that in many cases the bonds and alliances that are formed in the social or semi-social setting become increasingly important the higher you rise. They may lead to new opportunities, or help in the formation of a circle of people in similar roles whom you can bounce ideas off and whom you grow to trust. 'A lot of the friendship building, the networks, the support that frankly becomes really important when you start getting to the top, are being formed in ways that exclude women,' is Carolyn Fairbairn's view.[7] Even a brief after-work drinks reception may involve another few hours of expensive childcare and eat into precious family time – hard to justify if you don't know for sure that it's leading somewhere.

Indra Nooyi, who was one of the world's top business leaders through the years she ran PepsiCo, has addressed a fundamental issue that is hard to get away from. 'The biological clock and the career clock are in total conflict with each other. When you have to have kids you have to build your career. Just as you are rising to middle management your kids need you because they are teenagers. As you grow even more your parents need you because they are ageing.' And while she and her husband might feel they have done a decent job, the perspective of their children might be rather different. 'We plan our lives meticulously so we can be decent parents. But if you ask our daughters, I am not sure that they will say I have been a good mom.'[8]

I've tried to make my own choices with as much freedom as possible from the most unhelpful of sentiments – guilt. From feeling inadequate in comparison with the dedication of my own mother, wondering how I could model myself upon her and yet hand over my children and go out to work, I am now at peace with that – her time and mine are very different. I hope simply that I have been able to make as many good calls as possible when there have been priorities to gauge and judgements to make. Often those are about the everyday, but sometimes life comes at you in a way that makes starkly clear what is important and what is not.

In the autumn of 2016, not long after I had begun writing this book, the cancer treatment that my father had been undergoing for the past four years stopped being effective in keeping the disease at bay. My mother, brother and I witnessed his weakness and pain increasing and realised there was little time remaining when he refused further treatment, saying 'the end result will be the same'.

But there was also a strange and somehow beautiful balance in it all. It hit me the first day I lifted his feet to help him into the passenger seat of the car as we drove to a hospital appointment. I imagined all the times in years long past that he would have lifted me up as a baby and a child. And it was there again every time I arrived at my parents' home in the early hours of the morning in those final weeks, to take over from my mother who would have been up with him during the night. A decade before, it was my newborn babies she would have been handing back into my arms after looking after them for me overnight.

Muslims are taught that only three things remain of a person after they are gone: an ongoing act of charity, knowledge from which others benefit, and the prayers of a righteous child. I like to think that my father made a continuing gift of knowledge because he bequeathed his body to medicine, so that students might learn about anatomy in the way he himself had done. In the last few days I overheard him telling my mother she was the love of his life – words I had never before heard him say. And it was probably only in that period that I truly understood the full weight of how my parents shaped me and what their commitment to my education made possible. My father was generally bemused, however, by my various work–life–family dilemmas, saying only 'You'll work it out', when I voiced them. I think of them more as a work in progress. But that's good enough for me.

In Brief

A formula for saying no

The adage 'if you need something done, ask a busy person' means that an organised, effective individual is likely to get swamped with myriad requests. Work out a formula to sift through these – for example, you might decide to say yes to those that benefit you at work, help out your children's school, or those that might build contacts for something you want to do in the future. A year later, your formula might be different as your priorities and interests change, but unless you have limitless time on your hands, you will need to have a swift and effective way of deciding what to take on and what to politely decline.

The formula should apply whatever the time-frame

It is all too easy to put something in the diary for months ahead, only to feel a sense of dread as it approaches. Therefore your formula should be applied consistently whether the request is one for next week or next year.

Review and rethink rather than feel guilty

Guilt is understandable when you're juggling multiple balls, but it is not going to help manage the demands or work out a better way to deal with them. Redirect yourself away from it and towards a more constructive approach. Is there one project or aspect of your life from which you can excuse yourself or do less of for a while, until you have more capacity?

Work on the bonds that pay dividends in a crisis

Look out for the ways in which you can step in and help out colleagues or fellow parents at the school gates, when you are able to. These are circles of trust and appreciation that can make an immense difference when you are up against it – but you have to be prepared to be on the giving side, too.

Afterword

Over the period of time that I spent on this book, gender in the workplace acquired an urgency that I could not have predicted when I set out on the project. At the beginning, I was primarily occupied with the practical – the tried and tested strategies and approaches that had helped me make sense of the ups and downs of my professional path, as well as what I had gleaned from others. Achieving your potential in the workplace was, I believed, largely an individual mission. Unless you were up against a particularly adverse set of circumstances or at the whim of an exploitative employer, it should be within your grasp.

Then came gender pay reporting, Me Too and the BBC pay row – all contributing to conversations of unprecedented candour between colleagues, both women and men. High pay and equal pay, progression and stagnation, opportunities and barriers – all of this began to be discussed and debated in a way I had never previously experienced. 'I didn't know anyone else felt the same way' was a familiar refrain, soon becoming: 'If only we had talked like this years ago.'

My sense of individual mission became three-pronged as I thought increasingly about societal norms and expectations – and about the way our systems of work are structured. On both of the first two, the present age of awareness and determination is making a tremendous difference, as individual self-belief is strengthened and society's old expectations are challenged. But the third is likely to continue to be a stumbling block. The structural barriers that can adversely affect women in combining a career with family life include rigidity in working patterns that force people to cut down what they do or quit; the cost and availability of childcare; the part-time or flexible options that can sideline workers and leave them disproportionately penalised on pay; and the professions where success is defined by making it to a certain level – such as partner in a law firm – by a certain age.

Unless these are properly tackled, the pyramid pattern – equal numbers of men and women coming into a particular industry, profession or company but the women fading away the more senior the position – will be perpetuated. It is for this reason that I cannot entirely share the confidence of those who say 'It will all be different for our daughters'. If we don't fix these ways of working, they will hit the same old barriers.

Despite progress on society's expectations, I also worry that in the years ahead younger women will still come up against biases that affect how their capability at senior levels and their leadership potential are viewed in relation to their male peers. I hope I'm wrong – and that we start hearing the words 'distinguished', 'esteemed' or 'genius' as often deployed for women as men.

Where there has been progress, we should not lose sight of how it happened. 'Let's agree that things have improved over the last fifty years, even over the last twenty, and then let's start to ask why', wrote the author Kamila Shamsie in 2015. She was reflecting on the sea-change in publishing since 1991, when there was an all-male shortlist for the Booker Prize – a moment synonymous with a new determination to publish and recognise more women writers. By 2014, just under 40 per cent of books submitted by publishers to the same prize were by women.[1] By 2017, women dominated a list of the UK's bestselling authors of literary fiction.[2] 'Was it simply the passage of time?' asked Shamsie. 'Should we all sit around while the world continues on its slow upward trend towards equality? Or should we step outside that fictional narrative of progress and ask what actually helped to change literary culture in the UK?'

Alongside all of that, I still believe in the power – and the duty – of the individual to play their part, to the fullest extent possible. Just as we would devote time and energy to learning a new software program or going through a new training manual: how we communicate and present ourselves and our skills should be no less important. It means that however hard it feels at the start, we should take on the new challenge and give it our best shot. However anxiety-inducing a big moment or performance, we have to try to channel those nerves. However awkward we feel, we should be prepared to state our ambitions and achievements without embarrassment or apology. And however daunting the path ahead, we owe it to ourselves to push forward and help make the future different from – and better than – the present.

Acknowledgements

Many people played a role in making this book a reality, starting with the person with whom I first discussed the idea: my friend and literary agent Elly James. I was fortunate to have her wise counsel throughout and can say for certain that without her, it would never have come to fruition.

Thank you to my publisher Louise Haines for her guidance and the wealth of experience she brought to this project, as well as to the team at 4th Estate and HarperCollins, including Sarah Thickett, Patrick Hargadon, Iain Hunt, Helena Caldon, Matt Clacher and Julian Humphries, who designed the cover.

Special thanks to Gilly Orr, formerly of *Today*, who helped with research and the development of ideas from the early stages right through to the very end. I am also grateful to Lorna Stewart, Harriet Noble, Hannah Sander and Lesley Todd.

Thank you to those who read the text or fed in thoughts in other ways: Malcolm Balen, Cathy Bor, Stephen Brecker, Tyler Brûlé, Elizabeth Day, Clare Elsmore-Dodsworth, Claudia Hammond, Louise Heywood, Sarah Montague, Mariana Panayides, Rohini Pande, Gemma Perlin, Francesca Segal, Harriet Tyce, Philip Watson and the 'BBC Women' group.

Thank you to my colleagues at *Today* and the *BBC News at Ten* and my editors there, Sarah Sands and Paul Royall. I'll also always be grateful to my first editor at *Today*, Jamie Angus.

Elsewhere, my heartfelt thanks to Joanna Kaye, Tracey MacLeod and the team at KBJ, to Iluminada Hizon for her help at home and her perennial good nature, and to three wonderful women who are always there for me: Nusrat Hashmi, Shahnaz Jafar and my mother Shama Husain.

To three men of the future: Rafa, Zaki and Musa, may you grow up to be wise, considerate and kind.

And to my husband Meekal: thank you for your support for this book, despite the time it took away from our shared life. I owe you more than I can say.

Notes

Introduction

1. Catalyst, *Pyramid: Women in S&P 500 Companies (February 2, 2018)*. http://www.catalyst.org/knowledge/women-sp-500-companies

2. Research by INvolve, released March 2018. Reported in Elizabeth Pfeuti, 'Daves Still Outnumber Female CEOs in FTSE 100', *Financial News*, 8 March 2018. https://www.fnlondon.com/articles/daves-still-outnumber-female-ceos-in-ftse-100-20180308

3. Frequently Asked Questions: MPs. UK Parliament website. https://www.parliament.uk/about/faqs/house-of-commons-faqs/members-faq-page2/#jump-link-3

4. As reported to the Solicitors Regulation Authority: https://www.sra.org.uk/sra/equality-diversity/key-findings/law-firms-2017.page

5. Research by Professor Lis Howell of City University into the *ITV News at Ten*, *BBC News at Ten*, Radio 4's *Today*, *Channel 4 News*, *5 News* and *Sky News Sunrise*. https://www.city.ac.uk/news/2018/june/women-on-air-research

6. Research by Engineering UK 2018. https://www.wes.org.uk/content/wesstatistics

7. *Newsnight*, BBC Two, 12 October 2017

8. Lesley Stahl, 'Leading by Example to Close the Gender Pay Gap', CBS News, 15 April 2018. https://www.cbsnews.com/news/salesforce-ceo-marc-benioff-leading-by-example-to-close-the-gender-pay-gap/

the skills

Where We Are

1. Women in National Parliaments, 2018 figures. Compiled by the Inter-Parliamentary Union. http://www.ipu.org/wmn-e/classif. htm

2. 'Reality Check: Does China's Communist Party Have a Woman Problem?' BBC News, 25 October 2017. http://www.bbc.co.uk/ news/world-asia-41652487

3. Women in Business: Beyond Policy to Progress, report by Grant Thornton International Ltd, March 2018. https://www. grantthornton.co.uk/globalassets/1.-member-firms/global/ insights/women-in-business/grant-thornton-women-in-business-2018-report.pdf

4. Marcus Noland, Tyler Moran and Barbara Kotschwar, 'Is Gender Diversity Profitable? Evidence from a Global Survey', Working Paper Series. WP 13-3. February 2016. Peterson Institute for International Economics. https://piie.com/system/ files/documents/wp16-3.pdf

5. Vivian Hunt, Sara Prince, Sundiatu Dixon-Fyle and Lareina Yee, 'Delivering through Diversity', January 2018. http://www. mckinsey.com/business-functions/organization/our-insights/ delivering-through-diversity

6. Global Gender Gap Report 2017. World Economic Forum. http://reports.weforum.org/global-gender-gap-report-2017/ key-findings/

7. Sage Lazzaro, 'It Will Take 170 Years for Women to Be Paid the Same as Men', Observer.com, 26 October 2016. http://observer. com/2016/10/it-will-take-170-years-for-women-to-be-paid-the-same-as-men/

8. Rohini Pande, 'Getting India's Women into the Workforce: Time for a Smart Approach', Ideas for India, 10 March 2017. https://www.povertyactionlab.org/sites/default/files/2017.03.10-Pande-I4I.pdf

9. Rohini Pande and Charity Troyer Moore, 'Why Aren't India's Women Working?' *New York Times*, 23 August 2015. https:// www.nytimes.com/2015/08/24/opinion/why-arent-indias-women-working.html

10. Ibid.
11. Speaking on the *Today* programme, BBC Radio 4, 21 February 2018
12. Amelia Gentleman, '"I'm Beyond Anger" – Why the Great Pay Gap Reveal Is an Explosive Moment for Gender Equality', *Guardian*, 23 February 2018. https://www.theguardian.com/ news/2018/feb/28/gender-pay-gap-reveal-explosive-moment- equality
13. ONS figures for 2017; https://visual.ons.gov.uk/ explore-the-gender-pay-gap-and-test-your-knowledge/
14. Monica Costa Dias, Robert Joyce and Francesca Parodi, 'Wage Progression and the Gender Wage Gap: The Causal Impact of Hours of Work', February 2018. https://www.ifs.org.uk/ publications/10364
15. Claudia Goldin, 'How to Achieve Gender Equality in Pay', *Milken Institute Review* (2015), July (Q3): 24–33. https://scholar. harvard.edu/files/goldin/files/gender_equality.pdf
16. Nick Triggle, 'Top Women Doctors Lose Out in NHS Pay Stakes', BBC News, 16 February 2018. http://www.bbc.co.uk/ news/health-43077465
17. Full report here: http://downloads.bbc.co.uk/aboutthebbc/ insidethebbc/reports/pdf/annex_annual_report_201617.pdf. NB the list excluded payments made by commercial entities such as BBC Worldwide and payments made by independent producers
18. Lewis Goodall, 'The BBC Gender Pay Gap Is Bad – But Its Class Gap Is Worse', Sky News, 23 July 2017. https://news.sky.com/ story/the-bbc-pay-gap-is-bad-its-class-gap-is-worse-10957166
19. 'City Grandee Leading Campaign for Women to Rise to the Top in Business Says BBC Women Were Paid Less', *Evening Standard*, 27 July 2017
20. Lesley Stahl, 'Leading by Example to Close the Gender Pay Gap', CBS News, 15 April 2018. https://www.cbsnews.com/news/ salesforce-ceo-marc-benioff-leading-by-example-to-close-the- gender-pay-gap/
21. Tim Worstall, 'Finally, People Are Getting It Right About the Gender Pay Gap', Adam Smith Institute, 23 November 2017.

https://www.adamsmith.org/blog/finally-people-are-getting-it-right-about-the-gender-pay-gap

22. 'How Iceland is Fighting the Gender Pay Gap', BBC World Hacks, 17 October 2017. http://www.bbc.co.uk/programmes/w3csv3hv

23. Jenny Steinitz, 'Major Gender Gap in History Tripos', *Cambridge Student*, 9 February 2015. http://www.tcs.cam.ac.uk/news/0033788-serious-gender-gap-in-history-tripos.html; Examination results and degrees statistics 2015, Cambridge University: https://www.prao.admin.cam.ac.uk/files/es_2015_corrected.pdf

24. Statistical information on the University of Oxford: http://www.ox.ac.uk/gazette/statisticalinformation/#d.en.6208

25. V. Gibson, L. Jardine-Wright and E. Bateman, 'An Investigation into the Impact of Question Structure on the Performance of First Year Physics Undergraduate Students at the University of Cambridge', *European Journal of Physics*, 36 (2015) 045014. http://www.hep.phy.cam.ac.uk/~gibson/Women%20in%20Science/EurJPhys-36-2015-045014.pdf

26. Sathnam Sanghera, 'Elitism, the Oxbridge Access Problem – And Why I Never Felt I Belonged at Cambridge', *The Times*, 14 April 2018. https://www.thetimes.co.uk/article/sathnam-sanghera-elitism-the-oxbridge-access-problem-and-why-i-never-felt-i-belonged-at-cambridge-8dtm77jvf

27. D. Z. Grunspan, S. L. Eddy, S. E. Brownell, B. L.Wiggins, A. J. Crowe and S. M. Goodreau 'Males Under-Estimate Academic Performance of Their Female Peers in Undergraduate Biology Classrooms', *PLOS One* (2016) 11(2): e0148405

28. E. Zschirnt and D. Ruedin, 'Ethnic Discrimination in Hiring Decisions: A Meta-Analysis of Correspondence Tests 1990–2015' (5 August 2015), *Journal of Ethnic and Migration Studies*, January, 1–19, 2016; https://papers.ssrn.com/sol3/papers.cfm?abstract_id=2597554

29. Martin Wood, Jon Hales, Susan Purdon, Tanja Sejersen and Oliver Hayllar, 'A Test for Racial Discrimination in Recruitment Practice in British Cities', a report of research carried out by National Centre for Social Research on behalf of the

Department for Work and Pensions, 2009. http://www.natcen. ac.uk/media/20541/test-for-racial-discrimination.pdf

30. Vivienne Ming, 'The Hidden Tax on Being Different', *HR Magazine*, 23 November 2016. http://www.hrmagazine.co.uk/ article-details/the-hidden-tax-on-being-different

Growing Up Female

1. 2017 survey; https://www.girlguiding.org.uk/globalassets/docs-and-resources/research-and-campaigns/girls-attitudes-survey-2017.pdf

2. L. Bian, S. J. Leslie and A. Cimpian, 'Gender Stereotypes About Intellectual Ability Emerge Early and Influence Children's Interests', *Science* (2017), 355, 389–91; research summary here: http://mindsetscholarsnetwork.org/wp-content/uploads/ 2017/03/Cimpian_Gender_Stereotypes_Develop_Early.pdf

3. Ben Schmidt, Northeastern University, www.benschmidt.org. http://benschmidt.org/maps-visualizations-gallery/

4. Claire Cain Miller, 'Is the Professor Bossy or Brilliant? Much Depends on Gender', *New York Times*, 6 February 2015. https:// www.nytimes.com/2015/02/07/upshot/is-the-professor-bossy-or-brilliant-much-depends-on-gender.html

5. Michelle King, 'Geena Davis is Creating Opportunities for Women in Hollywood by Tackling Gender Bias', *Forbes*, 3 April 2017. https://www.forbes.com/sites/michelleking/2017/04/03/ geena-davis-is-creating-opportunities-for-women-in-hollywood-by-tackling-gender-bias/4/#6a314cc24b71

6. Dr Stacy L. Smith and Crystal Allene Cook, 'Gender Stereotypes: An Analysis of Popular Films and TV', Geena Davis Institute on Gender in Media. https://seejane.org/wp-content/uploads/GDIGM_Gender_Stereotypes.pdf; https://seejane.org/research-informs-empowers/gender-in-media-the-myths-facts/

7. See www.dykestowatchoutfor.com/the-rule

8. '100 Women: How Hollywood Fails Women on Screen', BBC News, 2 March 2018. http://www.bbc.co.uk/news/world-43197774

9. Hanah Anderson and Matt Daniels, 'Film Dialogue from 2,000 Screenplays, Broken Down by Gender and Age', The Pudding, April 2016. https://pudding.cool/2017/03/film-dialogue/

10. Dr Stacy L. Smith, Marc Choueiti and Dr Katherine Pieper with assistance from Yu-Ting Liu and Christine Song, 'Gender Bias Without Borders: An Investigation of Female Characters in Popular Films Across 11 Countries', Geena Davis Institute on Gender in Media. https://seejane.org/wp-content/uploads/gender-bias-without-borders-full-report.pdf

11. Martha M. Lauzen, 'It's a Man's (Celluloid) World: Portrayals of Female Characters in the 100 Top Films of 2017', https://womenintvfilm.sdsu.edu/wp-content/uploads/2018/03/2017_Its_a_Mans_Celluloid_World_Report_3.pdf; and Martha M. Lauzen, 'The Celluloid Ceiling: Behind-the-Scenes Employment of Women on the Top 100, 250, and 500 Films of 2017', 2018. https://womenintvfilm.sdsu.edu/wp-content/uploads/2018/01/2017_Celluloid_Ceiling_Report.pdf, both Center for the Study of Women in Television and Film, San Diego State University, 2018

12. Lucinda Coxon, 'Representing Women', talk for International Women's Day 2016.

13. Melissa Silverstein, 'Firing Harvey Weinstein Was a Start, But Hollywood Needs a Revolution', Women and Hollywood, 12 October 2017. https://blog.womenandhollywood.com/firing-harvey-weinstein-was-a-start-but-hollywood-needs-a-revolution-23171bef1229

14. Léa Seydoux, '"I had to Defend Myself": The Night Harvey Weinstein Jumped On Me', *Guardian*, 11 October 2017. https://www.theguardian.com/commentisfree/2017/oct/11/harvey-weinstein-lea-seydoux

15. Jennifer Perry and Katie Booth, 'Reese Witherspoon Might Be Right About Her "Most Hated Question"', Women in the World, 13 November 2015. https://womenintheworld.com/2015/11/13/reese-witherspoon-might-be-right-about-her-most-hated-question/

16. Monica Hesse and Dan Zak, 'Violence. Threats. Begging. Harvey Weinstein's 30-Year Pattern of Abuse in Hollywood', *Washington*

Post, 14 October 2017. https://www.washingtonpost.com/lifestyle/
style/violence-threats-begging-harvey-weinsteins-30-year-
pattern-of-abuse-in-hollywood/2017/10/14/2638b1fc-aeab-
11e7-be94-fabb0f1e9ffb_story.html?utm_term=.
fb06a63006bb

17. Chimamanda Ngozi Adichie, 'We Should All Be Feminists',
TEDxEuston, December 2012. https://www.ted.com/talks/
chimamanda_ngozi_adichie_we_should_all_be_feminists/
transcript

18. 'Are Pakistan's Female Medical Students to Be Doctors or
Wives?', BBC News, 28 August 2015. http://www.bbc.co.uk/
news/world-asia-34042751

19. Z. Hazari et al, 'Factors that Affect the Physical Science Career
Interest of Female Students: Testing Five Common Hypotheses',
Physical Review Special Topics – Physics Education Research
(2013), vol. 9. https://journals.aps.org/prper/pdf/10.1103/
PhysRevSTPER.9.020115

20. Speech to the annual conference of the Girls' Day School Trust,
14 June 2016. https://www.gdst.net/article/channelling-your-inner-
cheerleader

Planning

1. Carl Benedikt Frey and Michael Osborne, 'The Future of
Employment: How Susceptible Are Jobs to Computerisation?',
Oxford Martin School at the University of Oxford. https://www.
oxfordmartin.ox.ac.uk/downloads/academic/future-of-
employment.pdf

2. Mrs Moneypenny with Heather McGregor, *Mrs Moneypenny's
Careers Advice for Ambitious Women* (Penguin Random House,
2012), p. 96

3. Lynda Gratton and Andrew Scott, *The 100-Year Life: Living and
Working in an Age of Longevity* (Bloomsbury, 2016)

4. Sarah Harper, *How Population Change Will Transform Our
World* (Oxford University Press, 2016)

5. Professor Sarah Harper, 'The 21st Century: The Last Century of
Youth', Oxford Institute of Ageing, London lecture, 2012:

https://www.youtube.com/watch?v=JpsYA4G9uP0; also, an interview on *Today*, 20 February 2018

6. Speaking on *Today*, 20 February 2018
7. Nick Chambers, Dr Elnaz T. Kashefpakdel, Jordan Rehill and Christian Percy, 'Drawing the Future', Education and Employers, January 2018. https://www.educationandemployers. org/wp-content/uploads/2018/01/DrawingTheFuture.pdf
8. Caroline Leaper, 'Miriam González Durántez On Why All Women Should Be Inspiring Others @Work', *Marie Claire*, 8 April 2016. http://www.marieclaire.co.uk/life/work/ miriam-gonzalez-durantez-clegg-inspiring-women-71818
9. Girls' Attitude Survey 2016, Girlguiding, p. 37. https://www. girlguiding.org.uk/globalassets/docs-and-resources/research-and-campaigns/girls-attitudes-survey-2016.pdf
10. Penny de Valk, 'You Plan Your holiday, So Why Not Your Career?' *Guardian*, 17 June 2013. https://www.theguardian. com/women-in-leadership/2013/jun/17/plan-your-holiday-why-not-your-career
11. BBC Radio's *Test Match Special* with Ed Smith, 11 August 2016

Preparation

1. Remarks by the president at Commencement Address, Rutgers, the State University of New Jersey, The White House of President Barack Obama. https://obamawhitehouse.archives. gov/the-press-office/2016/05/15/remarks-president-commencement-address-rutgers-state-university-new
2. See for example Google founders' 2004 letter: https://abc.xyz/ investor/founders-letters/2004/ipo-letter. html#_ga=2.215983185.732231449.1527258002-1985481093.1527258002
3. Eli Pariser, 'Beware Online "Filter Bubbles"', Ted2011. https:// www.ted.com/talks/eli_pariser_beware_online_filter_bubbles/ transcript#t-416873
4. 'How News Feed Works', Facebook. https://www.facebook.com/ help/327131014036297/

5. Dave Lee, 'Facebook, Twitter and Google Berated By Senators on Russia', BBC News, 1 November 2017. http://www.bbc.co.uk/news/technology-41837435

6. Zeynep Tufekci, 'What Happens to #Ferguson Affects Ferguson: Net Neutrality, Algorithmic Filtering and Ferguson', Medium, 14 August 2014. https://medium.com/message/ferguson-is-also-a-net-neutrality-issue-6d2f3db51eb0

7. Joseph Harker, 'Stop Calling the Calais Refugee Camp the "Jungle"', *Guardian*, 7 March 2016. https://www.theguardian.com/commentisfree/2016/mar/07/stop-calling-calais-refugee-camp-jungle-migrants-dehumanising-scare-stories

8. Eric Lubbers, 'There Is No Such Thing as the Denver Guardian, Despite That Facebook Post You Saw', *Denver Post*, 5 November 2016. https://www.denverpost.com/2016/11/05/there-is-no-such-thing-as-the-denver-guardian/

9. Alison Kershaw, 'School Children "Should Be Taught to Recognise Fake News"', *Independent*, 18 March 2017. http://www.independent.co.uk/news/uk/home-news/school-children-taught-recognise-fake-news-donald-trump-andreas-schleicher-a7636251.html

10. Vice-Chancellor's admission address, University of Oxford, 12 January 2016. http://www.ox.ac.uk/news/2016-01-12-vice-chancellors-admission-address

11. 'Ten Things You May Not Know About Wikipedia', Wikipedia. https://en.wikipedia.org/wiki/Wikipedia:Ten_things_you_may_not_know_about_Wikipedia

12. Jonathan Head, 'Myanmar Conflict: Fake Photos Inflame Tension', BBC News, 2 September 2017. http://www.bbc.co.uk/news/world-asia-41123878

13. 'Corbyn Facts', *More or Less*, BBC Radio 4, 28 August 2016. http://www.bbc.co.uk/programmes/b07pjkj5

14. Nathaniel Cramp, 'Vinyl Indignity: Record Sales Are Up, But Small Labels Don't See the Benefit', *Guardian*, 9 December 2016. https://www.theguardian.com/music/musicblog/2016/dec/09/vinyl-record-sales-up-but-indie-labels-dont-see-benefit

15. Ibid.

16. C. Vlachopoulos et al., 'Electronic Cigarette Smoking Increases Aortic Stiffness and Blood Pressure in Young Smokers', *Journal of the American College of Cardiology* (2016), vol. 67, issue 23, June. http://www.onlinejacc.org/content/67/23/2802

17. 'Vaping in England: Evidence Update Summary', February 2019. www.gov.uk

18. Roger Dean Deakin, 'How Campbell's Soup's Former CEO Turned the Company Around', Fast Company, 18 September 2014. https://www.fastcompany.com/3035830/how-campbells-soups-former-ceo-turned-the-company-around

Starting Out

1. R. Rosenthal and L. Jacobson, 'Pygmalion in the Classroom', *Urban Review* (1968), 3(1), pp. 16–20. https://www.uni-muenster.de/imperia/md/content/psyifp/aeechterhoff/sommersemester2012/schluesselstudiendersozialpsychologiea/rosenthal_jacobson_pygmalionclassroom_urbrev1968.pdf

2. L. Jussim and K. Harber, 'Teacher Expectations and Self-Fulfilling Prophecies: Knowns and Unknowns, Resolved and Unresolved Controversies', *Personality and Social Psychology Review* (2005), 9(2), pp. 131–55. http://www.rci.rutgers.edu/~jussim/Teacher%20Expectations%20PSPR%202005.pdf

3. Carol S. Dweck, 'The Secret to Raising Smart Kids', *Scientific American*, 1 January 2015. https://www.scientificamerican.com/article/the-secret-to-raising-smart-kids1/

4. C. I. Diener and C. S. Dweck, 'An Analysis of Learned Helplessness: Continuous Changes in Performance, Strategy, and Achievement Cognitions Following Failure', *Journal of Personality and Social Psychology* (1978), 36(5), pp. 451–62. http://dx.doi.org/10.1037/0022-3514.36.5.451; http://psycnet.apa.org/record/1979-13073-001

5. Interviewed for the HBR IdeaCast, *Harvard Business Review*, 2012

6. L. Blackwell, K. Trzesniewski and C. Dweck, 'Implicit Theories of Intelligence Predict Achievement Across an Adolescent Transition: A Longitudinal Study and an Intervention', *Child*

Development (2007), 78(1), pp. 246–63. http://mtoliveboe.org/cmsAdmin/uploads/blackwell-theories-of-intelligence-child-dev-2007.pdf

7. Sal Khan, 'The Learning Myth: Why I'll Never Tell My Son He's Smart', Khan Academy. https://www.khanacademy.org/talks-and-interviews/conversations-with-sal/a/the-learning-myth-why-ill-never-tell-my-son-hes-smart

8. Katherine Forster, 'At 48, and with My Three Boys Growing Up Fast, I'm the New Office Intern'. *Spectator*, 9 September 2017. https://www.spectator.co.uk/2017/09/at-48-and-with-my-three-boys-growing-up-fast-im-the-new-office-intern/

9. I. Bohnet, *What Works: Gender Equality By Design* (Harvard University Press, 2016)

10. Athene Donald, 'Conspiracy or Cock-up?' blog post, 3 February 2017. http://occamstypewriter.org/athenedonald/2017/02/03/conspiracy-or-cock-up/

11. Gardiner Morse, 'Designing a Bias-Free Organization', *Harvard Business Review*, July–August 2016. https://hbr.org/2016/07/designing-a-bias-free-organization

Speaking Up

1. 'A Conversation with Christine Lagarde', Centre for Strategic and International Studies, 7 March 2017. https://www.youtube.com/watch?v=LdwfTRzdrD4

2. 'Let Her Speak' documentary presented by Emily Maitlis, BBC Radio 3, November 2016. http://www.bbc.co.uk/programmes/b081t4vt

3. 'Spoken Like a Woman' presented by Anne Karpf, *Archive on 4*, BBC Radio 4

4. Jean Seaton, *Pinkoes and Traitors: The BBC and the Nation 1974–1987* (Profile, 2015)

5. Speaking on *Today*, 31 December 2014

6. Deborah Cameron, *The Myth of Mars and Venus* (Oxford University Press, 2007)

7. Deborah Cameron, 'Just Don't Do It', blog, 4 July 2015. https://debuk.wordpress.com/2015/07/05/just-dont-do-it/

8. Mishal Husain, 'Can a Robot Do My Job Better Than Me?' *Mail on Sunday*, 31 December 2017. http://www.dailymail.co.uk/news/article-5223829/MISHAL-HUSAIN-robot-job-better-me.html

9. India Knight, 'Don't Be So Hard On Yourselves, Ladies, Silence Your Inner Critic', *Sunday Times*, 26 June 2016. https://www.thetimes.co.uk/article/india-knight-dont-be-so-hard-on-yourselves-ladies-silence-your-inner-critic-3w36k8msm

10. Elizabeth Day, *Paradise City* (Bloomsbury, 2015)

11. Elizabeth Day, 'Can Writing a Male Character Make You Think Like a Man?' The Pool, 11 April 2015. https://www.the-pool.com/archive/life/life-honestly/2015/14/can-writing-a-male-character-make-you-think-like-a-man

12. *Woman's Hour*, BBC Radio 4, 3 July 2015. http://www.bbc.co.uk/programmes/b060brht

13. Interview with Emily Maitlis on BBC *Newsnight*, 7 September 2016

Standing Up

1. 'What Trump's Hand Gestures Say About Him', BBC News, 16 August 2016. http://www.bbc.com/news/av/election-us-2016-37088990/what-trump-s-hand-gestures-say-about-him; MH interview with Mary Civiello

2. Deborah Gruenfeld, 'Power and Influence', Stanford Graduate School for Business, YouTube, 13 March 2013. https://www.youtube.com/watch?v=KdQHAeAnHmw

3. Marianne Cooper, 'For Women Leaders, Body Language Matters', 15 November 2010. https://gender.stanford.edu/news-publications/gender-news/women-leaders-body-language-matters

4. Mary Civiello, 'The DeVos Smile ... Nothing to Smile About', LinkedIn, 12 March 2018. https://www.linkedin.com/pulse/devos-smilenothing-smile-mary-civiello

5. A. Mehrabian, *Silent Messages: Implicit Communication of Emotions and Attitudes* (Wadsworth, 1981), pp. 51–2 http://www.kaaj.com/psych/smorder.html

6. Mehrabian, *Silent Messages*, pp. 51–2

7. Ibid., p. 54
8. 'Madrid Cracks Down on "Manspreading" on Public Transport', BBC News, 10 June 2017. http://www.bbc.co.uk/news/world-europe-40233435
9. I. Young, 'Throwing Like a Girl: A Phenomenology of Feminine Body Comportment Motility and Spatiality', *Human Studies* (1980), 3(1), pp. 137–56.
10. J. Willis and A. Todorov, 'First Impressions: Making Up Your Mind after a 100-ms Exposure to a Face', *Psychological Science* (2006), 17(7), pp. 592–8. http://journals.sagepub.com/doi/abs/10.1111/j.1467-9280.2006.01750.x
11. N. Ambady, R. Rosenthal and R. Geen, 'Half a Minute: Predicting Teacher Evaluations From Thin Slices of Nonverbal Behavior and Physical Attractiveness', *Journal of Personality and Social Psychology* (1993), 64(3), pp. 431–41. https://ambadylab.stanford.edu/pubs/1993Ambady.pdf
12. Malcolm Gladwell, *Blink: The Power of Thinking Without Thinking* (Penguin, 2006)
13. Author interview with Jo Palmer-Tweed
14. D. R. Carney, A. J. C. Cuddy and A. J. Yap, 'Power Posing: Brief Nonverbal Displays Affect Neuroendocrine Levels and Risk Tolerance', *Psychological Science* (2010), 21(10), pp. 1363–8. http://www.people.hbs.edu/acuddy/in%20press,%20carney,%20cuddy,%20&%20yap,%20psych%20science.pdf

The Digital You

1. 'Gay Times Editor Rivers "Appalled" By His Own Comments', BBC News, 16 November 2017. http://www.bbc.co.uk/news/entertainment-arts-42012079
2. Laura Hughes, 'Labour's Stoke Candidate Apologises to Wife and Daughter for Describing Women as "Polished Turds"', *Daily Telegraph*, 21 February 2017. https://www.telegraph.co.uk/news/2017/02/21/labours-stoke-candidate-apologises-wife-daughter-describing/
3. Kate Imbach, 'Fairytale Prisoner by Choice: The Photographic Eye of Melania Trump', Medium, 16 April 2017. https://

medium.com/@kate8/fairytale-prisoner-by-choice-the-photographic-eye-of-melania-trump-f1f7b97fff29

4. Louise Ridley, 'Change.org President Jennifer Dulski Says Women Start Fewer Petitions But They Win More Often', Huffington Post, 6 March 2015. http://www.huffingtonpost.co.uk/2015/03/06/changeorg-jennifer-dulski-women-petitions_n_6817132.html

5. 'Stop Taxing Periods. Period. #EndTamponTax', Change.org. https://www.change.org/p/george-osborne-stop-taxing-periods-period

6. 'United Airlines: Shares Drop After Passenger Dragging Video', BBC News, 11 April 2017. http://www.bbc.co.uk/news/world-us-canada-39563570

7. Addy Dugdale, 'Crib Sheet: Natalie Massenet, Founder of Net-a-Porter', Fast Company, 4 February 2010. https://www.fastcompany.com/1605214/crib-sheet-natalie-massenet-founder-net-porter

8. Google Diversity Report 2019 and Facebook 2019 Diversity Report

9. Maxine Williams, Global Director of Diversity, 'Facebook Diversity Update: Building a More Diverse, Inclusive Workforce. More About Our People, Programs and Progress in 2017', Facebook, 2 August 2017. https://newsroom.fb.com/news/2017/08/facebook-diversity-update-building-a-more-diverse-inclusive-workforce/

10. Susan Fowler, 'Reflecting On One Very, Very Strange Year at Uber', blog post, 19 February 2017. https://www.susanjfowler.com/blog/2017/2/19/reflecting-on-one-very-strange-year-at-uber

11. Re-Search: Makes Image Search Gender Balanced. https://semcon.com/re-search/

12. T. W. Bolukbasi, V. Saligrama, K. Chang, J. Zou and A. Kalai, 'Man Is to Computer Programmer as Woman Is to Homemaker? Debiasing Word Embeddings', Advances in Neural Information Processing Systems (2016), pp. 4356–64.

13. Author interview with Barbara Grosz via email; Will Knight, 'How to Fix Silicon Valley's Sexist Algorithms', MIT Technology

Review, 23 November 2016. https://www.technologyreview. com/s/602950/how-to-fix-silicon-valleys-sexist-algorithms/

14. Anasuya Sengupta, 'Where On the Internet is Your Knowledge?' Awid Women's Rights, 26 August 2016. https://www.awid.org/ news-and-analysis/where-internet-your-knowledge

15. 'BBC 100 Women 2016: How to Join Our Edit-A-Thon', BBC News, 7 December 2016. http://www.bbc.co.uk/news/ technology-38219838

16. Yvette Cooper, 'Why I'm Campaigning to Reclaim the Internet from Sexist Trolls', *Daily Telegraph*, 26 May 2016. http://www. telegraph.co.uk/women/politics/why-im-campaigning-to-reclaim-the-internet-from-sexist-trolls/

17. Simon Hattenstone, 'Gina Miller: "The Dishonesty Still Goes On. That's What I Abhor"', *Guardian*, 13 May 2017. https:// www.theguardian.com/politics/2017/may/13/gina-miller-interview-article-50-brexit-tactical-voting

18. Jon Ronson, *So You've Been Publicly Shamed* (Picador, 2015)

19. Barkha Dutt, 'Online Abuse a Weapon to Silence Women', *Hindustan Times*, 19 April 2017

20. 'How Russian Bots Appear In Your Timeline', BBC News, 14 November 2017. http://www.bbc.co.uk/news/technology-41982569; 'Trove of "Russian Troll" Posts Exposed by Congress', BBC News, 2 November 2017. http://www.bbc.co.uk/news/ technology-41844025

Keeping Sharp

1. Speaking to the *Guardian*, 4 February 2002: https://www. theguardian.com/film/2002/feb/04/artsfeatures and to *Gramophone*, 20 February 2017: https://www.gramophone. co.uk/feature/john-williams-interview-its-not-hard-work-that-makes-success-its-sustained-hard-work-that

2. Matthew Syed, 'Should People Accept that Pressure Is a Fact of Life?' BBC News, 1 May 2012

3. Speaking to *Stylist* magazine, February 2015

4. Jessamy Calkin, 'Maggie Smith On the Real Lady in the Van: "Nobody Will Ever Understand Why She Ended Up Like That"',

Daily Telegraph, 24 December 2016. https://www.telegraph.
co.uk/films/0/maggie-smith-real-lady-van-nobody-will-ever-
understand-ended/

5. 'Eleanor Roosevelt', FDR Presidential Library and Museum.
   https://fdrlibrary.org/eleanor-roosevelt

6. Eleanor Roosevelt, *The Autobiography of Eleanor Roosevelt*
   (1962; Da Capo Press, 1992)

7. Interview with Dinah Rose QC

8. J. D. Dodson and R. M. Yerkes, 'The Relation of Strength of
   Stimulus to Rapidity of Habit-Formation in the Kitten', *Journal
   of Animal Behaviour* (1915), 5(4), pp. 330–6

9. David H. Barlow, *Anxiety and Its Disorders: The Nature and
   Treatment of Anxiety and Panic* (Guildford Press, 1988)

10. 'Work-Related Stress, Depression or Anxiety', Health and Safety
    Executive. http://www.hse.gov.uk/statistics/causdis/stress/

11. Caitlin Moran, *Moranifesto* (Ebury, 2016)

12. 'Can Cognitive Behavioural Therapy Really Change Our
    Brains?', BBC iWonder. http://www.bbc.co.uk/guides/
    z2vfyrd#zp4rcdm

13. An interview with Aaron Beck on CBT, Philosophy for Life, 27
    April 2011. http://www.philosophyforlife.org/an-interview-
    with-aaron-beck-on-cbt/; 'Stoicism and REBT, the Philosophic
    CBT Model', College of Cognitive Behaviour Therapists.
    http://www.cbttherapies.org.uk/2013/11/19/stoicism-and-rebt-
    the-philosophic-cbt-model/

14. Margaret Graver, 'Epictetus', *Stanford Encyclopedia of Philosophy*
    (Summer 2017 Edition), edited by Edward N. Zalta. https://
    plato.stanford.edu/archives/sum2017/entries/epictetus/

15. Claudia Hammond, *Emotional Rollercoaster* (HarperCollins,
    2010)

16. Katherine Woollett and Eleanor A. Maguire, 'Acquiring "the
    Knowledge" of London's Layout Drives Structural Brain
    Changes', *Current Biology* (2011), 21(24), pp. 2109–14. https://
    www.ncbi.nlm.nih.gov/pmc/articles/PMC3268356/

17. Ian Robertson, *The Stress Test: How Pressure Can Make You
    Stronger and Sharper* (Bloomsbury, 2016)

notes

Owning It

1. Patti Smith, 'How Does It Feel', *New Yorker*, 14 December 2016

2. I. Bohnet, *What Works: Gender Equality by Design* (Harvard University Press, 2016), and interview by Jeff Guo in *Washington Post*, 16 March 2016

3. Hannah Riley Bowles, Linda Babcock and Lei Lai, 'Social Incentives for Gender Differences in the Propensity to Initiate Negotiations: Sometimes It Does Hurt to Ask', *Organizational Behavior and Human Decision Processes* (2007), 103(1), pp. 84–103. https://www.cfa.harvard.edu/cfawis/bowles.pdf

4. B. Artz, A. H. Goodall and A. J. Oswald, 'Do Women Ask?' *Industrial Relations: A Journal of Economy and Society*, Cass Business School, University of Warwick and University of Wisconsin (2016). https://www2.warwick.ac.uk/fac/soc/economics/research/workingpapers/2016/twerp_1127_oswald.pdf

5. Jennifer Lawrence, 'Why Do I Make Less Than My Male Co-Stars?', Lenny Letter, 14 October 2015. https://us11.campaign-archive.com/?u=a5b04a26aae05a24bc4efb63e&id=64e6f35176&e=1ba99d671e#wage

6. Speaking to *Marie Claire*, January 2017. http://www.marieclaire.co.uk/entertainment/natalie-portman-admits-to-this-male-actor-being-paid-more-than-her-465954

7. A Conversation with Linda Babcock and Sara Laschever, Women Don't Ask. http://www.womendontask.com/questions.html; Linda Babcock, Sara Laschever, Michele Gelf and Deborah Small, 'Nice Girls Don't Ask', *Harvard Business Review*, October 2003. https://hbr.org/2003/10/nice-girls-dont-ask

8. Mrs Moneypenny with Heather McGregor, *Mrs Moneypenny's Careers Advice for Ambitious Women* (Penguin Random House, 2012)

Rising Up

1. Juliet Eilperin, 'White House Women Want to Be in the Room Where It Happens, *Washington Post*, 13 September 2016. https://www.washingtonpost.com/news/powerpost/wp/2016/09/13/white-house-women-are-now-in-the-room-where-it-happens/?utm_term=.fd2200abc5e0

2. Mary Beard, *Women and Power: A Manifesto* (Profile Books, 2017)

3. Bridie Jabour, 'Julia Gillard's "Small Breasts" Served Up on Liberal Party Dinner Menu', *Guardian*, 12 June 2013. https://www.theguardian.com/world/2013/jun/12/gillard-menu-sexist-liberal-dinner

4. 'Julia Gillard's "Misogyny Speech" In Full', ABC News, YouTube, 8 October 2012. https://www.youtube.com/watch?v=ihd7ofrwQX0

5. Laura Bates, 'Julia Gillard's Views on Sexism in Politics Are About Every Woman in Every Job', *Guardian*, 16 June 2015. https://www.theguardian.com/lifeandstyle/womens-blog/2015/jun/16/julia-gillards-views-on-sexism-in-politics-are-about-every-woman-in-every-job

6. Quoted in Liza Mundy, 'Playing the Granny Card', *The Atlantic*, June 2015. https://www.theatlantic.com/magazine/archive/2015/06/playing-the-granny-card/392105/

7. S. Fiske, A. Cuddy, P. Glick, J. Xu and P. Devine, 'A Model of (Often Mixed) Stereotype Content: Competence and Warmth Respectively Follow From Perceived Status and Competition', *Journal of Personality and Social Psychology* (2002), 82(6), pp. 878–902.

8. Apoorva Sripathi, 'Sagarika Ghose on How Lurid Misogyny Contributed to How We See Indira Gandhi Today', The Ladies Finger!, 12 July 2017. http://theladiesfinger.com/sagarika-ghose-indira-gandhi/

9. 'Iron Lady Frightens' by Yuri Gavrilov, described by historian Dominic Sandbrook in *Strange Days: Cold War Britain*, BBC, 2014. https://www.bbc.co.uk/education/clips/z969d2p

10. Speaking on *Today*, 20 April 2018; Caroline Slocock, *People Like Us, Margaret Thatcher and Me* (Biteback, 2018)

11. Interviewed on NBC, September 2017. https://www.today.com/news/hillary-clinton-was-dumbfounded-former-fbi-director-s-pre-election-t116229

12. Susan Chira, 'Why Women Aren't CEOs, According to Women Who Almost Were', *New York Times*, 21 July 2017. https://www.nytimes.com/2017/07/21/sunday-review/women-ceos-glass-ceiling.html?mcubz=1&_r=0

13. Dylan Byers, 'Turbulence at the Times', *Politico*, 23 April 2013. http://www.politico.com/story/2013/04/new-york-times-turbulence-090544

14. Marianne Cooper, 'For Women Leaders, Likability and Success Hardly Go Hand-in-Hand', *Harvard Business Review*, 30 April 2013. https://hbr.org/2013/04/for-women-leaders-likability-a

15. M. Ryan and S. Haslam, 'The Glass Cliff: Evidence that Women Are Over-Represented in Precarious Leadership Positions', *British Journal of Management* (2005), 16(2), pp. 81–90

16. Lillian Cunningham, 'Christine Lagarde: "Don't Let the Bastards Get You"', *Washington Post*, 12 July 2014. https://www.washingtonpost.com/business/on-leadership/lagarde-on-leadership-its-about-encouraging-people/2014/07/11/4696f284-06b5-11e4-a0dd-f2b22a257353_story.html?utm_term=.2f856b37add3

17. Margaret Hodge, 'How to Stop Wasting Women's Talents: Overcome Our Fixation with Youth', *Guardian*, 23 August 2016. https://www.theguardian.com/commentisfree/2016/aug/23/wasting-women-talent-youth-balance-family-career

18. Interviewed in *Newsweek*, 24 April 2009. http://www.newsweek.com/chiles-michelle-bachelet-surviving-crisis-77289

Resilience

1. Andrew Pierce, 'Day the BBC's Golden Girl Became a Spokesman for Corbyn: On a Miserable Week for Presenter Mishal Husain', *Daily Mail*, 6 June 2017. http://www.dailymail.co.uk/news/article-4578830/ANDREW-PIERCE-miserable-week-BBC-s-Mishal-Husain.html

2. Interviewed by Nigel Smith for the *Guardian*, 19 August 2016. https://www.theguardian.com/film/2016/aug/19/30-minutes-with-natalie-portman-tale-of-love-and-darkness

3. Speaking at the Women In The World Summit, 3 April 2014. http://time.com/49751/hillary-clintons-best-advice-for-succeeding-in-a-mans-world/

4. Maria Konnikova, 'How People Learn to Become Resilient', *New Yorker*, 11 February 2011. https://www.newyorker.com/science/maria-konnikova/the-secret-formula-for-resilience

5. E. Werner, 'Risk, Resilience, and Recovery: Perspectives from the Kauai Longitudinal Study', *Development and Psychopathology* (1993), 5(4), pp. 503–15

6. Interviewed on *Woman's Hour*, BBC Radio 4, 4 November 2015; Brené Brown, *Rising Strong: The Reckoning. The Rumble. The Revolution* (Ebury, 2015). http://www.bbc.co.uk/programmes/b06myrjm

7. Katty Kay and Claire Shipman, *The Confidence Code* (HarperCollins, 2014)

8. J. Wood, W. Perunovic and J. Lee, 'Positive Self-Statements: Power for Some, Peril for Others', *Psychological Science* (2009), 20(7), pp. 860–6

9. Ted Hughes, *Letters of Ted Hughes*, selected & edited by Christopher Reid (Faber & Faber, 2007)

Balance

1. Interview with Judi Casey and Karen Corday. http://www.flexiblework.umn.edu/MoenSloan_Network_News_InterviewSept-2009.pdf

2. P. Moen and S. Sweet, 'From "Work–Family" to "Flexible Careers"', *Community, Work & Family* (2004), 7(2), pp. 209–26

3. 'Work-life Fit and the Life Course', Network News, Sloan Work and Family Research Network, September 2009, vol. 11(9). http://www.flexiblework.umn.edu/MoenSloan_Network_News_InterviewSept-2009.pdf; https://www.bizjournals.com/twincities/news/2011/04/06/u-of-m-study-best-buy-flextime-turnover.html

notes

4. Jo Swinson, 'Why I'm Not Running to Be Lib Dem Leader', *Spectator*, 18 June 2017. https://blogs.spectator.co.uk/2017/06/jo-swinson-im-not-running-lib-dem-leader/

5. 'Ruth Bader Ginsburg's Advice for Living', *New York Times*, 1 October 2016. https://www.nytimes.com/2016/10/02/opinion/sunday/ruth-bader-ginsburgs-advice-for-living.html

6. Interview with the *Independent*, 23 November 2015. http://www.independent.co.uk/news/business/news/black-tie-business-dinners-should-make-way-for-more-female-friendly-events-says-cbi-chief-a6744456.html

7. Ruth Sunderland, 'Working Mothers Who Skip Boozy Dinners to See Family Don't Get Top Jobs Because They Can't Network to Get Ahead, Says CBI Chief', *Daily Mail*, 23 November 2015. http://www.dailymail.co.uk/news/article-3329722/Working-mothers-skip-boozy-dinners-family-don-t-jobs-t-network-ahead-says-CBI-chief.html

8. Speaking to David Bradley at the Aspen Festival, July 2014. https://www.theatlantic.com/business/archive/2014/07/why-pepsico-ceo-indra-k-nooyi-cant-have-it-all/373750/

Afterword

1. 'Kamila Shamsie: Let's Have a Year of Publishing Only Women – A Provocation', *Guardian*, 5 June 2015. https://www.theguardian.com/books/2015/jun/05/kamila-shamsie-2018-year-publishing-women-no-new-books-men

2. Tom Tivnan, 'Women Dominated the Top Literary Bestsellers Last Year', *Bookseller*, 15 January 2018. https://www.thebookseller.com/insight/atwood-leads-woman-dominated-literary-top-10-707621

Image credits

p. 26 From 'Explore the Gender Pay Gap and Test Your Knowledge', Office for National Statistics. https://www.ons.gov.uk/employmentandlabourmarket/peopleinwork/earningsandworkinghours/articles/explorethegenderpaygapandtestyourknowledge/2017-10-26

p. 46 From Ben Schmidt's interactive chart exploring the words used to describe male and female teachers in fourteen million reviews from RateMyProfessor.com. http://benschmidt.org/maps-visualizations-gallery

p. 80 Search engine results with kind permission from Eli Pariser.

p. 143 EMT manspreading sign, Madrid. http://www.emtmadrid.es/getattachment/e2157bbe-9b8f-4fc3-9b48-2348b901f048/NP-4517-MANSPREADING-SENALETICA-12-06-17.aspx

p. 143 MTA manspreading sign, New York. http://web.
mta.info/nyct/service/CourtesyCounts.htm

p. 211 *Vanity Fair* photograph © Sam Jones/Trunk
Archive.

p. 215 From Fiske, Cuddy, Glick and Xu, 'A Model of
(Often Mixed) Stereotype Content: Competence and
Warmth Respectively Follow From Perceived Status
and Competition', *Journal of Personality and Social
Psychology* (2002), vol 82, p. 885. http://www.people.
hbs.edu/acuddy/2002,%20fiske,%20cuddy,%20
glick,%20%26%20xu,%20JPSP.pdf

Epigraph sources

page 17: 'Each generation must create its own reality and find its own identity', Camille Paglia, from interview in Spiked, December 2015, http://www.spiked-online.com/spiked-review/article/feminist-trouble/17688#.Wyt9CS2ZOb8

page 41: 'We say to girls, you can have ambition, but not too much. You should aim to be successful, but not too successful', Chimamanda Ngozi Adichie, *We Should All Be Feminists* (4th Estate, 2014), p. 27

page 59: 'Progress depends on the choices we make today for tomorrow', Hillary Clinton, speech in Chicago, 27 August 1996

page 75: 'It is a narrow mind which cannot look at a subject from various points of view', George Eliot, *Middlemarch* (1871–2), Chapter 7

page 93: 'No matter what your current ability is, effort is what ignites that ability and turns it into accomplishment', Carol Dweck, *Mindset: The New Psychology of Success* (Random House, 2006)

page 115: 'The human voice is the most perfect instrument of all', Arvo Pärt, from interview in *Gramophone*, 7 July 2016, https://www.gramophone. co.uk/feature/an-interview-with-arvo-pärt-and-his-closest-musical-collaborators

page 135: 'Those with a deep understanding of human body language will always be in a better position to interpret the feelings, motives and machinations of others', Desmond Morris, from interview on www. all-about-body-language.com, http://www.all-about-body-language.com/desmond-morris.html

page 153: 'The internet is the organising principle of our age', Martha Lane Fox, from her 2015 Dimbleby Lecture, http://www.bbc.co.uk/mediacentre/ speeches/2015/martha-lane-fox-dot-everyone

page 175: 'Fright can transform into petrol', Judi Dench, from interview in *Stylist* magazine, February 2015, https://www.stylist.co.uk/people/judi-denchs-advice-to-her-30-year-old-self-from-coping-with-fear-to-subverting-the-norm/22807

page 191: 'Training is the answer to a great many things. You can do a lot if you are properly trained and I hope I have been', Queen Elizabeth II, *Elizabeth R: Year in the Life of the Queen*, BBC documentary, 1992

(director: Edward Mirzoeff; writers: Antony Jay, Edward Mirzoeff)

page 207: 'The free bird leaps on the back of the wind … and dares to claim the sky', Maya Angelou, 'Caged Bird' from the collection *Shaker, Why Don't You Sing?* (Random House, 1983)

page 225: 'Remember to look up at the stars and not down at your feet', Professor Stephen Hawking, 2016 Starmus Festival lecture

page 239: 'Love is the only thing that we can carry with us when we go', Louisa May Alcott, *Little Women* (1868), Chapter 40 'The Valley of the Shadow'

Index

index

the skills

index

index